Eat like it matters

Food choice, nutrition and wellbeing in a capitalist food system

ISY MORGENMUFFEL

2017

Published by Active Distribution
BM Active London WC1N 3XX, England
www.activedistribution.org
Printed by Sto Citas, Zagreb
2017

ISBN 9781909798403

Food and society

We are what we eat – not just in terms of what nutrients do in our bodies, but because our food and how we organise its supply is so incredibly detrimental to how we relate to each other, our environment and society. With technological developments and political reorganisation on a global scale, our lifestyles, food supply and subsequently our diets have massively changed over the last century.

The narrative of the many things that are inequitable and just plain not working in our current food system is a familiar one, told in a number of recommended writings[1]. The conclusions, though, often sadly fall short of the surely obvious solution: reorganise the food system in its entirety, from the bottom up, within a general social revolution. Let's face it, revolution is a daunting task and doesn't seem imminently achievable, so 'realistic' food writers skirt the issue, emphasising changes that are compatible with capitalism, from growing the local economy and using consumer power to increasing the efficacy of smaller scale agriculture. However, revolutionary aims and desires - no matter how far fetched and utopian - can inform what you do today, and if we believe in social change, we should approach our messed up food system in the same critical way that we approach work, life, relationships, and struggle. Food is a political battlefield, and resisting corporate power and improving

---

1 Particularly: Michael Pollan, Raj Patel, Marion Nestle, Vandana Shiva, Colin Tudge.

how and what we eat a meaningful and worthwhile struggle.

The human food supply was pretty simple for much of our history, as we hunted and gathered and did a bit of food growing, largely sustainably[2], from our immediate environments with a usually adequate and often abundant supply of nutrients from a far wider range of sources than we enjoy today. In this *original affluent society* as the anthropologist Sahlins called it, all was in common. The gradual emergence of grain-based agriculture and the domestication of animals only 20 000 years ago completely changed our diets, lifestyle and society. It not only affected dietary diversity, human health and our impact on the environment; it also allowed for the growth of settlements into cities, and for a surplus of grain that could be owned, stored, and distributed, creating wealth and power. Some argue this was a deciding factor in the development of hierarchies within growing, settled, farming societies (e.g. Richard Manning in *Eating Fossil Fuels* (2006)).

2 See Marshall Sahlins (1972) *Stone Age Economics*. A note here on the idea of humans living in balance with nature in a simpler society – although from what we know this seems on the whole true, this was also often a learning process, and indiscriminate forest clearing (even pre-agriculture) or uncontrolled hunting had a significant impact on the environment. Just one example from the excellent *'Green History of the World'* (Clive Ponting, 1991) is Madagascar, where within just a few hundred years of its settlement, many of the larger animals, including a pygmy hippo!, were extinct as they made such easy hunting.

4

Straw.   ferries

Alongside the establishment and growth of capitalism, food supplies became globalised with trade, colonial expansion, and the cultivation and exchange of new crops over the ages of seafaring and empires. In the West, we discovered our taste for sugar, coffee, potatoes and other imported goodies. The inventions of the steel plow, tractors, and mechanised farm machinery expanded the acreage farmers could cover. A whole new age then dawned in the middle of the 20th century with the development of a corporate food industry (supermarkets, multinational food producers) and, to the detriment of the environment, industrial agriculture. Faced with the perceived threat of peasant revolution and communism, the Rockefeller Foundation began a hybrid (crossbred and infertile) grain development programme in Mexico in 1941, a post-revolutionary country with a healthy agricultural output[3]. The aim was to increase yields and wrest back control over agricultural production. These new varieties grew faster and were more productive, mostly thanks to increased tolerance for fertilisers and pesticides. While this 'Green Revolution' has been credited with dramatically increasing agricultural output – doubling cereal production between 1961-1985 - and averting famine, the reality is

---

3 Cullather, N (2010) *The Hungry World*

that the main areas it was first applied (India, Mexico, South East Asia) are all now areas suffering from high levels of malnutrition, and it's created a whole host of problems.

Industrial agriculture has a high input of resources – water, fertilisers and pesticides, technology and irrigation, much of which is fossil fuel dependent – with decreasing output over time. It's created the larger scale farms and the straight long rows of grains in monocultures that cover our countryside. Whereas agriculture was never exactly benign towards the environment, causing deforestation and soil erosion, it now had a lot more horsepower.

The same industrialisation process was also applied to keeping animals and even fishing. Increased yields of grains allowed us to lock animals up instead of keeping them in pasture, feed them grains and let them move little to speed up their growth into many cuts of meat. The intensification of animal farming is undoubtedly one of the most horrific and damaging aspects of our current food system. Have you ever been inside an egg battery farm? It will give you nightmares. Higher inputs and inefficient conversion of grain into meat and dairy mean the increased depletion of resources (soil, water, fossil fuels) and use of land as well as a huge contribution to climate change, especially considering the potency of methane (from cow farts) as a greenhouse gas. Keeping animals at close quarters means the blanket use of antibiotics and easy spread of disease. You've seen the images, and you know the cost of animal products today.

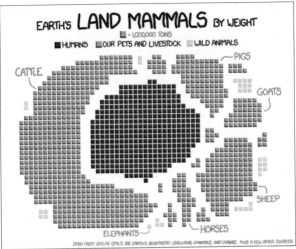

from xkcd.com

There are a lot of numbers bandied about and often exaggerated, or slightly misrepresented to make a point. However, it's clear that industrial animal agriculture has a significant impact in terms of human activity on this planet – by biomass alone (see xkcd graphic!), land use (nearly ¾ of the world's agricultural land), and resource use.

Greenhouse gas emissions contributed by animal agriculture are usually described with the FAO's estimate[4] of 18% (compared to the transport - 13%), which included a large percentage of the more potent greenhouse gases

---

4 Steinfeld et al (2006) *Livestock's Long Shadow*. FAO

methane and nitrous oxide (from cow farts, manure, and fertiliser application). A WorldWatch report included extra factors such as breathing and recalculated land use, and arrived at the figure of 51% of total emissions[5].

The figures for water and land use vary greatly, but it's generally agreed that agriculture as a whole is responsible for 70% or more of water use, and according to the FAO, grazing land and cropland for animal feed represents almost 80% of all agricultural land.

The idea that eating plants directly, rather than growing grains to feed to animals to then eat them, is a more efficient and both climate and environment friendly use of land is fairly obvious. It's of course a bit more complicated, e.g. when you compare pasture fed sheep to imported out of season apples, or consider that a lot of land used for grazing is unsuitable for crop production. But the reality of animal farming today is intensive feedlots, a large consumption of grain fed beef with its disproportionate use of water, land and inputs. Globally, about 80% of the soybean crop and a third of the cereal crop is fed to animals (Millstone and Lang (2008) *The Atlas of Food*).

Industrial agriculture developed alongside the growth of corporations and multinational food producers driven by a need to make profits, supermarkets, advertising and globalised trade. Our political and economic frameworks favour this large scale and industrial production of inferior

---

5 Goodland and Anhang (2009) *Livestock and Climate Change*. WorldWatch

food, distributed in a way to make rich countries richer and poor countries hungry. In a competitive capitalist food industry, it's not enough just to make a good product; capitalist growth demands new lines, new products, added value, cutting costs, and exploitative arrangements. We have ended up with a crazy food system that is not geared towards feeding us well or meeting our nutritional needs, farming sustainably or distributing food equitably. The expectations we have of food don't fit into the framework of the commodity. From cornershops selling us crap to agricultural wastelands, the list of what's wrong, inefficient, and unjust in how we produce our food is long.

FISHING

Fish consumption is increasing, and destructive fishing technologies such as bottom trawling, along with badly regulated and monitored fishing practises have resulted in very few sustainable fish stocks remaining, and most commonly eaten fish species are under pressure. Fish farming suffers from pollution and disease, and depends on wild fish stocks for feed and populations.

WATER & POLLUTION

Up to a mind boggling 5000 litres of water is needed to produce the daily food for just one person[6], and 70% of freshwater withdrawals is used by agriculture (especially irrigation). Climate change is also causing water scarcity. Run-off from manure, fertilisers and pesticides also affects water quality, from nitrite contaminated groundwater to dead zones in rivers and oceans, where excess phosphates have led to oxygen depletion.

---

6 Millstone and Lang (2008) The Atlas of Food

ENVIRONMENTAL RACISM

As with other aspects of capitalist society, it's the poor that are disproportionately affected by the pollution caused by industrial farming, e.g. animal factory farms or food processing plants are sited in poor rural areas[7].

FARMING

Although half of the world's population live in rural areas and 90% of the world's farms remain small scale (though squeezed onto only 25% of the world's farmland)[8], in the UK, the number of small farms declined by 11000 between 1987 and 2003[9]. Only 1% of the total workforce consists of agricultural workers (compared to for example 49% in Thailand or 75% in Uganda[10]).

FOSSIL FUELS & CLIMATE CHANGE

Our food system is hugely dependent on fossil fuels. Natural gas is used to make fertilisers, gas and oil for pesticides and herbicides, and oil used for farm machinery and food transport. It's vulnerable to fossil fuel depletion or rising prices, and with deforestation, soil degradation and methane from animals, industrial agriculture is a significant contributor to climate change.

WASTE

According to the Waste and Resources Action Programme (2008), nearly half of what's grown in Britain is thrown away, including UK consumers chucking a third of the food they buy!

CORPORATIONS

Food is big business, and there are a few key players whose policies, actions and products have huge effects on

---

7 www.foodispower.org

8 GRAIN (2014) Hungry for land

9 Campaign to protect rural England

10 Millstone and Lang (2008) The Atlas of Food

people's lives and our world, and who can put pressure on suppliers to cut costs, engage in destructive and unfair practises, and lobby governments. In 2013, Nestle made over $11 billion profit and employed around 330000 people[11]. The combined sales revenue of the top ten food corporations is $33 billion more than the combined GDP of the 75 poorest countries (Millstone and Lang, Atlas of Food 2008). The concentration of power is also increasing; while the 10 biggest seed companies had 30% of the market share in 1996, the 3 biggest controlled 50% in 2013[12].

BIODIVERSITY

Pre-Green Revolution, there were over 3000 rice varieties in the Philippines – two decades in, just two varieties dominated the landscape[13]. According to the FAO's Staple Foods document, just 15 crop plants provide 90% of the world's food energy intake! An estimated 75% of our crop genetic diversity has been lost over the 20th century, making us more vulnerable to outbreaks of crop failures, disease and pests. Agriculture also affects biodiversity in the wider rural landscape, through pesticide use and fertiliser run off, and the general effects of monoculture cropping.

SOIL DEPLETION

Globally, we're losing 75 billion tonnes of soil each year[14], and half of the topsoil on the planet over the last 150 years, according to the WWF. Between 1981-2003, productivity declined on 12% of land due to nutrient depletion, erosion and pollution[15].

11 Oxfam (2014) Behind the Brands

12 EcoNexus & BD (2013) Agropoly

13 Ibid.

14 Campaign to protect rural England

15 Millstone and Lang (2008) The Atlas of Food

PROCESSED FOOD

Processed foods 'add value' and make more profit. US American diets consist of 70% processed foods, including 20% fast food takeaways[16].

CHEAP FOOD

The average UK household spends only about 9% of its expenditure on food, down from 16% in 1984 and 33% in 1961[17].

GENETICALLY MODIFIED FOOD

Still not requiring labeling in the US, where soy, rapeseed and sugarbeet is often GM, they remain controversial, not only due to a lack of knowledge of their long term effects on human health and the environment, but also for consolidating seed companies' power, and because the majority of GM trait development focuses on increasing herbicide tolerance, allowing even more spraying.

EXPLOITATION OF WORKERS

Agricultural workers often suffer poor conditions, from health damaging exposure to pesticides to low pay and exploited migrant labour. The UK food industry relies on flexible, cheap, and preferably desperate workers, often from migrant backgrounds (70-80% of harvest labour, and 35% of food manufacturing), often in conditions bordering on slavery[18].

FOOD POVERTY

We may have full supermarket shelves and lots of cheap food in the UK, but for many, feeding their families remains a struggle. Oxfam estimate that over 2 million people in the UK are

16   Marketplace.org
17 http://www.food security.ac.uk and Family Expenditure Survey (1961)

18 F. Lawrence, The supermarket gamble may be up, Guardian 20/2/17; Joseph Rowntree, www.jrf.org.uk)

malnourished, and 3 million at risk. Over 500000 people are reliant on food parcels. 'Full fact' estimate that there about 1500 emergency food providers in the UK, and this provision is growing.

WORLD HUNGER

925 million people experience hunger, and another estimated billion suffer malnutrition[19]. In theory, worldwide food pro-duction should easily meet need, at a daily average of 2720kCal/per person[20] - hunger isn't caused by a lack of food, but by poverty and landlessness. Industrial agri-culture and a globalised food system exacerbate the problem by raising the cost of farming, and by forcing farmers to grow higher profit export crops[21].

---

19 Foresight (2011) Future of Food and Farming report

20 World Hunger Educational Service (2011)

21 Kimbrell (2002) The Fatal Harvest Reader

BIOFUELS

Between 2001-2011, world biofuel production increased 5x, with a particularly steep rise in 2007/8 triggering a rise in food prices, and resulting in further land grabs and deforestation[22]. Demand is set to rise even further with the EU Biofuels Directive.

TRADE

Any pretense of free trade creating a more efficient, responsive and equitable food system has clearly failed; the main benefitters have been corporations and rich countries who have secured their global dominance while prices for commodities produced in poor countries have fallen and the demands of structural adjust-ment programmes and the like have further cemented their exploitation and prevented attempts at food sovereignity. Between 1980 and 1998, 19 of the world's 25 poorest

---

22 FAO (2013) HLPE Report Biofuels and Food Security

countries experienced declining terms of trade – e.g. 70%, in Nigeria and Uganda[23].

HABITAT LOSS

Nearly 40% of the world land mass is already devoted to agriculture, according to the FAO, 90% of wildflower meadows in the UK have been lost since the 1940s[24], and 20% of the Brazilian Amazon rainforest since 1970.

FOOD MILES

A quarter of UK HGV transport is food transport (Foresight, Future of Food and Farming report), and an oft-quoted statistic is that a US meal has travelled an average of 1500 miles. Disconnecting us from seasonal limitations and local produce, the UK imports about 40% of its food, and only one in three apples we eat in the UK is grown here[25].

Food miles are only one contributor to the environmental impact of food production and may be outweighed by comparative advantage (e.g. more efficient land or energy use), but only in some cases.

PESTICIDES

Pesticide use has been linked to environmental problems such as bee colony collapse, and human health problems from headaches and ADHD to hormonal disruption and cancer. The WHO report 3 million cases of direct pesticide poisoning, and 250000 deaths a year.

SUPERMARKET POWER

We only have 8% of greengrocers in the UK compared to the 1950s, and just 4 supermarket retailers hold 73% of the market share.

23 New Internationalist (2004)

24 Foresight (2011) Future of Food and Farming report
25 DEFRA

Further reading:

Colin Tudge (2004) So Shall we Reap; Vandana Shiva (2000) Stolen Harvest; Sandor Ellis Katz (2006) The Revolution will not be microwaved

-------------------**RECIPES: Wild Foods**--------------------

The idea of going out and foraging for your supper is a very attractive one. It's also become a bit of a foodie cliché. But it remains a way of perceiving and appreciating the natural world around you, connecting with the seasons, and getting some good nutrition too.

Basic guidelines
Never overpick an area, take scissors or a knife and avoid pulling up roots. Don't pick from the side of the road (traffic fumes, herbicides). Wash well before use. Pick flowers and berries on a sunny day when their fragrance is at their best. Only pick what you are pretty sure of, and in the appropriate season.

I'm a lazy and unadventurous forager and have my regular little yearly cycle of activity based on what's fairly readily accessible and easy to prepare. Seasonal and local variations are common though, so keep your eyes open.

SPRING
Spring's my favourite time for foraging, especially after a long and bleak winter! There are especially lots of exciting and easy greens to pick (most of which taste better and are more digestible early in season).

Nettles: Surely your most ubiquitous wild food and best in the spring or early summer before they've flowered – later in the season they grow bitter. Young tops have the best flavour. They're very nutritious, with iron, other minerals and Vitamin A, and a diuretic i.e. make you wee so make sure you drink enough water!

You can use nettles like other greens in recipes – e.g. nettle risotto, steamed and mixed up with potato mash, or as a spinach substitute, and you can even eat it raw as a salad, pounding them with lemon juice and a bit of olive oil will take off the sting.

Nettle soup (for 6) :

2 onions
Celery (optional)
3 peeled potatoes
1 litre stock
Large bag nettles
nutmeg, salt and pepper
Soy or cashew cream (see p. 131)

Chop and cook 2 onions and maybe a stick of celery in oil until softened. Add 3 peeled and chopped potatoes, and cover with 1 litre of light stock. Bring to the boil and cook until the potatoes are breaking apart. Then wash and roughly chop a large bag of nettles and add, cooking for just a few minutes. Season to taste and add a pinch of nutmeg and a splash of soy or cashew cream if you like, then puree.

Spring greens for salad: There are lots of delicious greens and flowers you can pick to add flavour to your salads – easy ones to come by and identify include jack by the hedge (also known as garlic mustard), sorrel, salad burnet, and dandelion flowerheads and leaves. Pick young leaves, and dress them lightly with a sweetened balsamic or lemony dressing.

Sag Aloo with greens (for 6):

Bag of wild greens
3 large potatoes
1 tsp cumin seeds
veg oil and marge
2 small onions
2 tsp garam masala
2 tsp turmeric
fresh ginger
2 cloves of garlic

Pick a bag full of wild greens – nettles, ground elder, chickweed, rinse well and roughly chop. Cook a sag aloo by parboiling 3 large potatoes, chopped into bitesize chunks. Then cook 1 tsp cumin seeds in 1-2 tbsp veg oil and 1 tbsp marge, then add 2 small chopped onions and cook until browning. Add the potatoes, 2 tsp garam masala, 2 tsp turmeric, a small bit of chopped fresh ginger and 2 cloves of garlic, chopped. Cook over low heat taking care not to let it stick, if it does, add a splash of water. When the potatoes are cooked, add the greens and cook for another 5 minutes with the lid on, and season to taste.

Stirfried greens: Richard Mabey recommends cooking chickweed or other delicate spring greens by simply washing them, shaking off, and cooking in a pan with a dash of oil, seasoning, and some chopped spring onions. Stir fry until soft (5 minutes) and then serve with a squeeze of lemon and sprinkle of nutmeg.

Wild garlic: This grows lots of places with a damp shady ground, you'll notice the sharp smell of it in the woods in early spring! You can use them as a garlic replacement in most dishes (add finely chopped leaves at the end of cooking), as a garnish, in salads.

Pesto:

Bag of wild garlic
Handful of pine nuts, cashew seeds or walnuts
Salt and pepper
1/3 cup olive oil
Lemon juice

The classic wild garlic dish is of course pesto. Make a big jar and keep it in your fridge for up to 2 weeks. Wash a small bag (or a few large handfuls) of wild garlic and shake dry. Tear into pieces, then add to a food processor along with either a handful of pine nuts if you are rich, or a large handful of toasted cashew seeds or walnuts. Season, and start whizzing, adding 1/3 cup of olive oil as you go. A little squeeze of lemon juice helps with the bitterness. You can also add a bit of vegan parmesan if you have it.
Also try sorrel or nettle pesto (blanch the leaves briefly, then rinse with cold – and add a bit of garlic to the recipe).

EARLY SUMMER

Seaweeds: All seaweeds in the UK are edible and full of good minerals! Some taste better than others though. They're good year round but best iin May and June, gathered at low tide, by cutting them from rocks and stones leaving a decent root (avoid free floating seaweeds, as you don't know where they've been!). Wash very well before use.

Seaweeds can be dried and stored; thinly sliced for a salad (e.g. dulse), shredded and stir fried to crisp in oil, or added to soups and stews (they will thicken them and add nutrition).

Elderflower: Elderflowers are fragrant and flowery deliciousness. Plus, locally picked elderflowers will help build your resilience for hayfever. Use dried sprigs for teas, also good for colds.

Elderflower fritters (for 4-6):

100g plain flour
2 tbsp veg oil, plus frying oil
175ml sparkling water
1 tbsp sugar
12 elderflower heads

First, make a batter: Sift the plain flour into a bowl, then add 2 tbsp veg oil and sparkling water, bit by bit, stirring to draw the flour in. Add a tbsp of sugar, and leave to sit for a little while. Rinse up to 12 elderflower heads and shake to dry. Heat oil at least 1.5 inches deep in a deep pan or wok until fairly hot, then dip the heads into the batter and into the oil, holding by the stem. Press them up and down a bit to help them fry all round until crisp and brown, and leave to drain on some kitchen roll. Best eaten hot and with a drizzle of syrup of sprinkling of sugar! NB: This is not the healthiest dish in the world. But.. mmmh.

Elderflower Cordial:

25 elderflower heads
3 lemons
1 orange
1kg sugar
1 tsp citric acid

I've always used the River Cottage recipe to make cordial. For 2 litres of cordial, use 25 elderflower heads – shake them well, then put them in a large food grade bucket or bowl along with the zest of 3 lemons and possibly one orange. Cover with 1.5 litres of boiling water and leave overnight. Strain through muslin into a large saucepan, and bring gently to the boil along with sugar, citric acid, and the juice from the lemons and orange, and cook a few minutes. Pour into sterilised bottles.

Marsh samphire: This grows in marshland and muddy coastlines, looks alien and is delicious with a bit of an asparagus taste to it. Cut the tall shoots with scissors, rinse well and boil in water for 5-10 minutes, drain well and serve with a balsamic vinaigrette to dip or just some melted margarine. Scrape the fleshy part from the centre stalk with your teeth.

Watercress: Grows in running water – avoid stagnant water or waters running through pasture, and make sure you haven't ended up with 'fool's cress'. Pick the older, bigger ones and use them to make a tasty soup.

Watercress soup (for 6):

2 onions
margarine
2 tbsp flour
350ml light stock
600ml soy milk
large bag watercress
salt and pepper
Cashew or soy cream (see p. 131)

Chop and cook two onions in oil and a dob of marge until translucent. Make a roux with 2 tbsp flour, then work in 350ml light stock and about 600ml soy or other milk. Heat gently and simmer for 5 minutes. Meanwhile, blanch a large bag of watercress (about 500g) in boiling water, drain, rinse with cold water and squeeze out, then add it to the soup, season and puree with some cashew or soy cream.

(Alternatively, you can just make a potato based soup and cook the watercress in it towards the end, for 5 mins max. You can also add a bit of spinach if you don't have quite enough watercress).

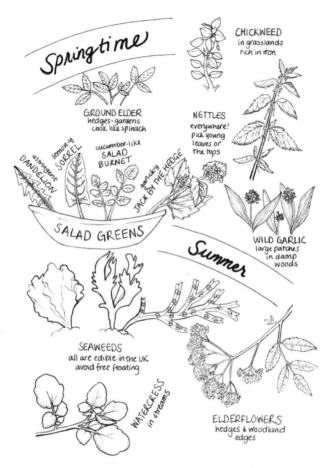

Springtime

CHICKWEED
in grasslands
rich in iron

GROUND ELDER
hedges · gardens
cook like spinach

NETTLES
everywhere!
pick young
leaves or
the tops

astringent DANDELION

lemony SORREL

cucumber-like SALAD BURNET

garlicky JACK BY THE HEDGE

SALAD GREENS

WILD GARLIC
large patches
in damp
woods

Summer

SEAWEEDS
all are edible in the UK
avoid free floating

WATERCRESS
in streams

ELDERFLOWERS
hedges & woodland
edges

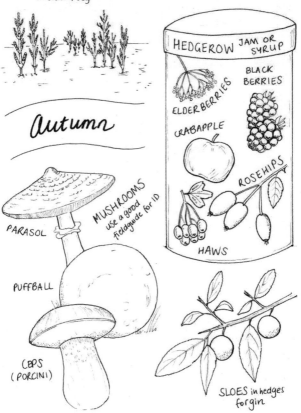

late summer: MARSH SAMPHIRE in coastal bog

HEDGEROW JAM OR SYRUP

ELDERBERRIES

BLACK BERRIES

CRABAPPLE

ROSEHIPS

HAWS

Autumn

MUSHROOMS
use a good
fieldguide for ID

PARASOL

PUFFBALL

CEPS
(PORCINI)

SLOES in hedges
for gin

23

LATE SUMMER

In the summer and autumn, my foraging focus turns to jam making and mushrooms. I like trying to build up a little store cupboard of goodies by the start of winter/for Christmas presents!

Crab apples: have grown directly from apple pips rather than being grafted, as commercial apples are, so they have unpredictable shapes and flavours. Many will be quite small and acidic, and make a nice jelly or addition to cider. You might also be lucky enough to come across some that are suitable for eating or cooking. There are so many things you can make with apples – add them to jam, apple pie/tarts, juice, use them in stews, apple crumble…

Blackberries: so ubiquitous in late summer, and so satisfying to pick a big bucket full and return home to make jam, pie, cordial, desserts.

Blackberry and apple jam:

2kg blackberries
1kg cooking
3kg white sugar

Adding a bit of apple to your blackberry jam increases the pectin content and so helps it set, making this an easy first time jam to try. Wash ripe blackberries, and peel and chop cooking apples. Heat in a small amount of water (not more than 400ml) in a pan (ideally not iron or aluminium) for anything from 15-45 minutes until pulpy. Add sugar, then bring to the boil slowly, stirring occasionally, and boil until it starts to set – this can be anything up to 20 minutes. To test if it's setting, put a small spoon on a cold plate, cool it down as quickly as possible, and if it has formed a skin after 1 minute, or if you draw a spoon through it and it remains separated, it's set. You can also test the temperature – setting point is usually at about 105°C. Remove from the heat, skim off any scum, and pack into sterilised jars. You should be able to eat it straight away.

AUTUMN
Elderberries: Take care, the stems and leaves are poisonous! It's easy to strip off the berries with a fork though and I've never had any trouble with them.

Winter syrup:

Large tub (about 700g) mixed berries
200g sugar
Whole spices
Muslin to strain

Syrups are relatively easy to make and come autumn, I start gathering hedge-row berries – haws, blackberries, rose-hips, and especially elderberries for their great immune boosting properties, and process them into my special Winter-Porridge-Syrup.
We have a clever Finnish stovetop steamer called a Mehu-maju to use – they're useful if you find one - but you

can also just use a heavy bottomed pan.

Heat a large tub of washed mixed berries in a pan with 200g/1 cup sugar and a bit of water (about 100ml). You can also add a few spices if you like, such as whole allspice, cinnamon, mixed spice. Bring gently to the boil, then simmer for about 30 minutes, until it's all pulpy. Stir often. Strain through muslin and fill into sterilised bottles.

You could also add echinacea or other herb tinctures to turn your syrup into a proper winter tonic.

Mushrooms: Mushroom foraging has an air of exclusivity (experienced mushroom hunters don't like to reveal their special spots, and then there's the constant threat of a false ID and poisoning yourself). However, it's not that difficult; some people are more open about the joys of mushrooms, and the best way is to go join someone who knows how and where to find some. The below are the ones I'm fairly confident about picking; there are a good few more and there's also regional variations. For a first find, it's worth picking a sample, taking it home and spending a bit of time on websites or with a good mushroom guide or two to get a proper ID (check gills, colour, where you picked it, any rings, colourings and staining, and maybe also a spore print). Then go back and get more if you found a good un!

If you pick lots, you can also slice and then dry mushrooms for later rehydrating and use; a proper dehydrator works best but a very low oven does the job too – it needs to be thorough though as they'll go mouldy if not.

Parasol Mushrooms: A fairly easily identifiable and distinguishable wild mushroom – but do make sure you got the right thing before you cook it. It's fairly prolific and grows quite large in open grassland, so a find of just a couple big ones will do for dinner. They're great just sliced into wedges and quickly fried for breakfast.

Ceps/Penny bun: Very much sought after and when you finally come across a fresh and gorgeous specimen you'll know why! Ceps have a lot of great flavour and are again fairly distinctive and identifiable, and are found in autumn in woodlands. They can grow quite large.

Giant puffball: One of the most distinctive wild mushrooms it literally looks a white giant puffball. Edible when it's creamy white throughout and has no gills. Grows in grasslands and delicious just thickly sliced and fried. Or use like you would tofu, or aubergine – it absorbs flavour in a similar way. Don't pick when it's not fresh looking, it will have produced spores or be close to.

Sloe Gin: Everyone and their dog makes sloe gin now. It's very easy: pick a bunch of sloes, prick them, add them to gin with a bunch of sugar (about half the weight of your sloes), leave to steep in a large jar and shake regularly for about 2 months, leave for another month then decant into a bottle. Approx. amounts would be 250g sugar, 500g sloes, 750ml gin. You can also try this with vodka, or with damsons, or even hawthorns.

Our Health

On the surface, Western societies and industrial capitalism seem to have been a huge success – but on closer inspection, you find that really, a lot of things just aren't working. We've been experiencing environmental problems, the gradual collapse of the financial system and various recessions, a shift to the right in politics (both parliamentary and in our everyday), crisis and war, and general instability. And despite an improved food supply, modern medical achievements and longer lives, we are, in all, not very well. The health problems we are suffering have changed since industrialisation and the emergence of a corporate and hierarchical medical system. It's claimed that we have 'conquered' infectious disease in the Western world (bar the occasional threat of a flu pandemic or outbreaks of diseases thought extinct such as tuberculosis or scarlet fever).

In a simplified narrative: before the enclosures of common land, European land-based peasants were doing fairly well apart from the odd plague. Then early capitalism and industrialisation and cities created the poor huddled and near-starving masses, dying of typhus and the like. Their lot improved over time and into the 20th century, with the emergence of public health and the discovery of sanitation, globalised exploitation and increasingly affluent Western societies. Today, it's the non-communicable (NCD, i.e. non-infectious) diseases and conditions that are mainly affecting Western people's lives and well-being. Cancer. Heart disease. High blood pressure (hypertension). Diabetes. Also, particularly, mental health issues, and neurodegenerative diseases such as Alzheimers. This is while poorer, colonised countries suffer both infectious disease AND the effects of imported Western lifestyles with increasing rates of diabetes and heart disease.

Heart disease

The term cardiovascular disease (CVD) describes any problems around the heart vessels, such as stroke, angina, and coronary heart disease involving blockages of the blood flow, usually due to atherosclerosis (a build up of plaque). Other heart diseases include infections (e.g. myocarditis), heart valve problems, or irregular heartbeat (arrhythmia). It's the number 1 cause of death globally (31% of deaths), affecting low and middle income countries the most.

Cancer

The harmful expansive mutation of cells, with causes ranging from exposure to carcinogenic substances, smoking, diet and lifestyle, genetics, infections, to radiation. The risk is ever increasing - up to 50% of those over 65 will suffer cancer in some form. In 2012, there were 14 million new cases globally, and 8.2 million cancer deaths.

Metabolic Syndrome

A term describing a cluster of 'risk factors', as the medical world love to classify and identify, for heart disease and diabetes. These include high blood sugar and insulin resistance (but not full blown diabetes), high blood pressure, high cholesterol levels and obesity.

Diabetes

A dysfunction of insulin, the hormone that regulates your blood sugar. This can either be Type 1, a serious lifelong condition in which your pancreas just doesn't produce any insulin, or Type 2, in which you make insulin but it doesn't work as effectively. Type 2 can develop at any time and has been on the rise as a result of Western lifestyles, but can also be improved with diet. The number of people with diabetes has risen 4x between 1980-2014 (108 million to 422 million).

Dementia and Alzheimers

Symptoms of impaired memory and brain function. Alzheimers progresses over time, and there is currently no cure. Globally, 44 million people have Alzheimers, with the highest prevalence in Western countries. 1 in 3 US Americans over 85 have Alzheimers.

Although the fact that we now live on average longer is certainly a reason for the shift toward NCDs, the more significant factors are down to the changes in lifestyle that we have seen in the last century. And this is much less to do with eating bad food or smoking or other naughty habits attributed especially to the poor, but to wider structural issues, including stress and poverty.

Especially evident is the increase in mental health problems. With varying degrees of severity, anxiety, depression and bipolar disorders affect so many of us, and struggling with your mental health is more the norm than the exception in Western societies today.

It doesn't help that we have a food system that sells us convenience and prioritises profits over our health, and a medical system that treats symptoms and individualises health problems without much willingness to consider the causes of disease. Modern medicine is more advanced than ever, but suffers from being corporate- and profit-driven, and there seems there is still very little it can do to combat chronic disease.

Weight and health

In public health and the public perception, obesity is seen as probably the biggest health burden. This isn't just an epidemic and illness that is challenging well-being, the obesity discourse is increasingly a moral one, laden with judgment and guilt, and inseparable from a whole host of other issues. Just think about the associations we have with obesity. Why do we think people are fat? We automatically assume it's because they eat too much, eat badly, and are lazy. It's seen as a marker of the decadence of an affluent capitalist society – it's often juxtaposed that there are 1 billion overweight people vs 1 billion malnourished in the world, as if the overweight people were directly snatching the sandwiches out of the hands of the hungry. Even many people who are concerned with equality and compassion speak with derision of obesity and pander to a thin ideal.

Obesity is not an abstract social problem, it's about people. Fat people face stigmatisation and discrimination, affecting their treatment in the workplace, education and in healthcare and their social status, and exacerbated by mass media[26]. There is also the inescapable fact that there is a social gradient in both health and obesity, and it tends to be poor people that are fatter, cementing inequalities, and making for uncomfortable classism when middle class professionals bemoan 'the obesity epidemic'.

Why are we so convinced that gluttony and sloth is some kind of default human state that needs controlling? That if left to our own devices and alone with a mountain of Twinkies, we just cannot help but eat all of them, every day, forever, until we collapse with a combination of heart disease, diabetes and cancer? The reality of why and how we are fat is not so simple.

Dominant myths around fatness have been challenged by critical researchers, such as whether fat is always unhealthy, or that permanent weight loss is achievable through dieting.

Body Mass Index (BMI) predicts mortality and morbidity: The BMI was developed to assess risk, a favourite pastime of

---

26 As documented extensively by Puhl and Brownell (2001) *Bias, Discrimination and Obesity.* Obesity 9 (12) and (2009) *The Stigma of Obesity, a review and update.* Obesity 17 (5).

our efficiency-seeking and categorising health service, and are fairly arbitrary lines drawn along your weight divided by your height. It doesn't take into account different builds or body shapes, muscle mass (which is heavier than fat), ethnic differences, or growth patterns in children. It also doesn't necessarily predict anything; e.g. in some studies, the 'overweight' category has been found to have the best longevity; it also has the most favourable rates of survival from cardiovascular disease. Flegal's US National Health and Nutrition Survey analysis found a relative ratio of mortality of 0.83 (i.e. a lower rate) for overweight compared to 'normal weight' amongst adults under 60[27].

Being fat makes you sick: Many diseases associated with obesity are not directly related but are metabolic issues - it's said that for example, larger people have high blood pressure (partly with the logic that if you're bigger, there's more blood to pump around?), or that fat cells (adipose tissue) are somehow inherently harmful. However there's plenty of 'metabolically healthy' overweight and obese people (25-35% of obese[28]), too many to just be an exception to the rule.

It's worth considering that our bias against, and our assumptions about obesity clouds research and findings; we look for causal links between obesity and disease,

---

27 Flegal et al (2005) *Excess Deaths Associated With Underweight, Overweight, and Obesity.* JAMA, Vol 293, No. 15.
28 Hankinson et al (2013) *Diet composition and activity level of at risk and metabolically healthy obese American adults.* Obesity 21(3).

when maybe we should be looking at factors such as physical activity, sugar consumption, metabolic function or stress levels instead. Obesity may also be the result, rather than the predictor of a disease condition, e.g. diabetes[29].

Our current approach to public health emphasises categorisation and risk. But risk factors are probabilities derived from a population, rather than an individual prediction; there are a lot of things at work in an individual's health and focusing on fat is usually not very helpful.

You have to be thin to be fit: This becomes a bit of a self fulfilling prophesy, as fatter people may feel judged and discouraged when wanting to engage in physical activity. It's clear though that physical activity and fitness is a better predictor for good health and longevity than just weight. Being overweight and fit carries half the relative risk of cardiovascular mortality than being 'normal weight' and unfit[30], and improving physical activity levels improves health, regardless of weight.

---

29 Campos, P. (2006) *The epidemiology of overweight and obesity: public health crisis or moral panic?* Int. Journal of Epidemiology 35(1).
30 Wei, M. *et al* (1999) *Relationship Between Low Cardiorespiratory Fitness and Mortality in Normal-Weight, Overweight, and Obese Men.* JAMA 282(16).

You can easily lose weight, you just need to persevere: Dieting for weight loss is ubiquitous, insidious, and has been shown to generally do more harm than good. Exacerbated by an appearance-focused society and the constant everyday judgment of each others bodies, quick-fix ways of losing weight are hugely appealing, and are pursued regardless of health. From fad diets and smoking to curb your appetite to disordered eating, dieting often results in unhealthy behaviours.

The issue is that you can't easily make your body lose weight in the long term. The obvious way is restricting how much you eat, but most bodies will compensate for this, slowing metabolism and storing more food eaten as fat. It's often quoted that 95% of dieters regain any weight lost over five years, and at least a third regain even more[31]. This sets people up for cycles of weight loss and gain, which has its own health implications (including an increased risk of heart disease, inflammation, and a higher mortality rate[32]). With all the odds stacked against you, trying to lose weight can turn into a vicious cycle, setting you up for failure and affecting self esteem.

---

31 e.g. Mann et al 2007, *Medicare's search for effective obesity treatments.* American Psychologist 62 (3)
32 S. Rosla et al (2016) *Risk of sudden cardiac death and coronary heart disease mortality in postmenopausal women with history of weight cycling.* American Heart Association Scientific Sessions; and Strohacker et al (2009) *Consequences of Weight Cycling: An increase in disease risk?* International Journal of exercise science 2 (3).

> It's estimated that 2/3 of adults suffer from negative body image
> 40% of under 10s worry about their weight
> The average age for girls to begin dieting is 8!
> One in 5 men have taken protein supplements to 'bulk up'
> 1 in 5 people in the UK have been victimised due to their weight
> 2/3 of women have avoided an activity (e.g. going to the beach, sport, for a job interview) due to feeling bad about their looks

APPG on Body Image (2012) Reflections on Body Image – Report
Etcoff et al (2006). Beyond stereotypes: Rebuilding the foundation of beauty beliefs: Findings of the 2005 global study. Dove.

Undoubtedly body fat, *when accompanied* by an unhealthy lifestyle, stress, and a lack of self care, is probably putting you on a course for ill health. However, the blanket assumption that all fat people are miserable, probably irresponsible and only have themselves to blame for anything terrible that befalls them, is prejudiced, harmful and generally unhelpful. Focusing on what people eat, their weight and their lifestyles - moral healthism emphasising personal responsibility – distracts from the broader social and economic issues that have an impact on well-being, and reinforces class divisions through moral judgment.

Health at every size (HAES) is a compassionate approach to healthcare that aims to shift the focus away from weight loss to health promotion. Its principles are:

1. Accepting and respecting the diversity of body shapes and sizes.
2. Recognizing that health and well-being are multi-dimensional and that they include physical, social, spiritual, occupational, emotional, and intellectual aspects.
3. Promoting all aspects of health and well-being for people of all sizes.
4. Promoting eating in a manner which balances individual nutritional needs, hunger, satiety, appetite, and pleasure.
5. Promoting individually appropriate, enjoyable, life-enhancing physical activity, rather than exercise that is focused on a goal of weight loss.   (ASDAH, 2013)

HAES both challenges dominant health practises and assumptions around obesity, and offers a way of working with individuals struggling with their weight, to learn to love themselves and engage in positive self care. Although mainstream health organisations are now putting more emphasis on healthy behaviours and cautioning against fad weight loss dieting too, the promise of benefiting from losing weight is still central to their approach. HAES takes this a step further, smashing the scales and looking at every individual's particular needs and situation, and how they can improve their lives. It's still fairly marginal, activist-based and does not have a huge evidence base, but what research there is has shown it is a successful approach, especially for those for whom dieting has 'failed'.

Further Reading:
Linda Bacon (2010), Health at Every Size

Diet and Health

Diet and health must be considered in a context. It's not like health is achieved by simply eating the right kinds of foods – so many things influence our health, including some that are out of our control, and food choice is just one factor. A factor that can be important, especially when we are looking for ways to improve our health, but for most people only one factor.

In the end, the major determinants for our well-being are social. Simply put, being lower class and lower status, experiencing discrimination and precarity, and being at the bottom of the social ladder is the biggest risk factor for most illnesses, especially metabolic conditions. The death rate is an average 2-3x higher for people at the bottom of a social hierarchy compared to those at the top.

The Whitehall studies of tens of thousands of British civil servants started in 1967, comparing mortality from disease in social classes. Even after controlling for other risk factors such as smoking or low levels of physical exercise, they still found higher mortality rates in the low grades compared to the high ones, especially for cardiovascular disease. Interestingly, these studies were of a socially and culturally quite similar group of people with stable incomes, but nevertheless found a strong social gradient in health. The research was developed further in the Marmot Review (2010), finding that people living in the poorest neighbourhoods in England had an average of 17 years more disability and 7 years shorter life expectancy than people in the richest areas.

Wilkinson and Pickett conducted a major survey of research relating to income inequality and health in different countries and areas, presenting their findings in accessible form in the groundbreaking book 'The Spirit Level' (2009). They also found that the correlations were not absolute but relative, i.e. it isn't how much money you have that has an effect on your health outcomes, but your social status in your society. The more unequal the society, the more health problems (as well as social problems, such as literacy or violent crime).

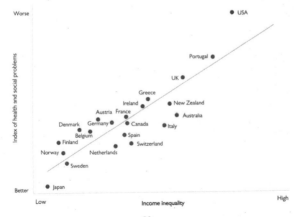

This suggests it isn't necessarily just due to material conditions such as access to healthcare or poor housing that we are ill, but to how we think and feel about our social status. This 'status anxiety' we experience in a hierarchical, unequal society – comparing ourselves to others, feeling judged, inferior and shame, being discriminated against, alongside worry over precarious/insecure conditions such as work or housing – causes stress and affects our health.

This social gradient in health is not just on class lines but also race or other marginalised differences. For example, incidence of hypertension is 2-3x higher in African Americans compared to white Americans[33].

The main mediator of this relationship between social status and health is probably stress. Our stress response involves hormonal reactions to a stressor. The adrenal glands secrete adrenaline and cortisol, which prepare the body for fight or flight by mobilising glucose and raising our blood sugar by inhibiting insulin, increasing our heart rate, and diverting energy from our digestive, immune and reproductive systems. This is a useful short term response for stress, but becomes deleterious to our health when the stressors are chronic – such as poor living/environmental conditions, pollution, or dietary factors, but also worry and anxiety or a feeling of vulnerability and powerlessness. Over time, this can affect our immune system, insulin response, inflammatory response, and sensitivity to

33 Kriefer and Sidney (1996) *Racial discrimination and blood pressure*. American Journal of Public Health 86

cortisol. Some individuals may have a healthy resilience to stress (influenced by genetics, early development, personality and also circumstance, social networks and support available), but it's clear that long term stress is a common experience in our society. As Linda Bacon puts it, we need to put nutrition in perspective, abandoning the approach of *"dieticians muscling in on people's lives with a lifestyle model of disease and a well-intentioned armory of behaviour change skills and calorie sheets, intent on teaching people how to cook with whole grains"*, and instead, looking at relationships and the big picture of health[34].

Further Reading:
Richard Wilkinson (2000) Mind the Gap. Darwinism Today series
Richard Wilkinson and Kate Pickett (2009) The Spirit Level

------------------**RECIPES: HEALTHY SNACKS**------------------

Juicing is basically removing the healthy fibre from fruit and veg and leaving the sugars. Smoothies on the other hand use the whole fruit and veg. Remember variety is key – you can have a shit ton of greens if you blend them, but a shit ton is not necessarily good for you, so mix things up. Go easy on any 'superfood additions' too – they're expensive anyway.

I like starting my day with a smoothie and it's a nice way of getting some fruit in, but smoothies shouldn't replace meals.

---

34 Linda Bacon (2006) *Eat Well, for yourself, for the world.*

Smoothie tips:
Put liquid in first to help it all get moving. Grate or chop up hard ingredients before adding, to help them break down. Start blending slow then speed it up, and blend for as long as you can – the smoother the better!
Nice little smoothie nutrition boosters include raw cacao nibs, hemp or linseeds, cinnamon, nuts or nut butters, or any of those overpriced superfood powders (don't use too much at a time, just add a teaspoon or even half – you might find them quite intense).

Green smoothie: Whizz a handful of greens (spinach or young kale), a pinch of nutmeg, and a cup of water or half water/half coconut milk. Then add half an avocado and whizz again.

Gloopy breakfast smoothie: Whizz 1 banana, handful of cashew nuts, 2 dates, 1/3 tin coconut milk, ½ cup water, 1 tbsp cocoa powder, plus ½ tbsp maca powder and a sprinkling of raw cocoa if you got.

Berry smoothie: Whizz 1 banana, a handful of ground almonds, a pinch of cinnamon and a handful of blue or other berries with some hemp/soy milk.

Nettle smoothie: Whizz 1 apple or kiwi, 1 banana or avocado, a large handful of nettle and of dandelion leaves (sub with some spinach if you don't have lots), 1 tsp wheatgrass powder (optional), the juice of half a lemon, and water to the desired consistency.

Bean dip:

Tin of beans
Olive oil
Garlic
Salt and pepper
Lemon or lime juice

Take a tin of beans or the equivalent of cooked beans – eg kidney, cannelini, pinto, etc. - drain and mash or blend with some olive oil, water, and flavourings: minced garlic, salt and pepper, lemon or lime juice. Extras include herbs, other spices, minced fresh chilli, chopped olives, a bit of tahini, nuts and seeds.

Butternut and tahini dip:

1 butternut squash
Salt, cinnamon
Olive oil
2-3 tbsp tahini
2 cloves garlic
Sugar
Lemon juice

Based on a recipe by Ottolenghi (who's cookbooks I much recommend). Peel and cut a squash into chunks, toss in a bowl with salt to taste, a sprinkle of cinnamon, and olive oil to coat and roast in a medium hot oven until soft; he recommends covering it with tinfoil and cooking for over an hour but I find less and uncovered is fine. When cooled, blend in a food processor with tahini, garlic, a pinch of sugar and a dash of lemon juice. Serve sprinkled with sesame seeds and fresh coriander.

Roasted nuts: Mix 2 cups of mixed whole nuts in a bowl with 1 teaspoon dark brown sugar, 2 teaspoons garam masala, a bit of salt and about 1 tablespoon of oil. Roast in a medium hot oven for 15-20 minutes.

Make your own mezze: Presented on a plate of pick and mix, even plain ol cucumbers actually become attractive! Try to keep a cupboard/fridge well stocked with healthy nibbles, here's some ideas:

Crackers and dips (hummous, bean dip) * Avocado slices * Nuts * Toasted seeds * Olives * Fresh vegetable crudites: carrot, cucumber and celery sticks, cherry tomatoes, radishes, thinly sliced beetroot (try the gorgeous candy beetroot!) * Tinned stuffed vine leaves or ready made falafel * Apple slices * Any steamed greens drizzled with olive oil

Raw veggie pate:

1 cup seeds	Soak seeds (sunflower, or ½ sunflower
1 carrot	½ pumpkin) for a few hours, then drain
1 stalk celery	and whizz in a processor with a carrot,
½ cup fresh herbs	celery, fresh herbs (coriander or
1 clove garlic	parsley), garlic, lemon juice and mellow
2 tbsp lemon juice	flavoured miso (eg white/cream
2 tbsp light miso	coloured). This recipe is from the
	wonderful *Get It Ripe* by Jae Steele.

Coconut chips: Toast a cupful of coconut chips/flakes (ideally organic) in a medium hot oven or in a dry hot pan for a few minutes, tossing a few times, until lightly browned. Remove, sprinkle with a pinch of salt and a pinch of cinnamon, and spread out to cool and become crunchy.
Variation: Toss first with some liquid smoke or smoke powder, 1-2 tbsp maple syrup, and a splash of tamari or soy sauce.

Oven roasted chickpeas:

1 tin chickpeas
1 tbsp oil
1 tsp garlic powder
salt, spices

Drain the chickpeas, and dry on a kitchen towel. Toss with oil, garlic powder, ½ tsp salt or less, and optional extra spices such as garam masala. Spread on a tray and roast in a medium oven (180 degrees) for 30-40 minutes, turning a couple of times.

Sushi (Korean-style):

350g sushi rice
50ml rice vinegar
2 tbsp sugar
Salt
Toasted sesame seeds
Veg for filling
5-8 nori sheets

Cook sushi rice to instructions. Heat vinegar, sugar and up to 1 tsp salt until it bubbles. Mix it into the cooked rice along with a tablespoon of toasted sesame seeds, and spread it out to leave to cool.

Fillings include strips of kimchi, cucumber or carrot strips (which you can pickle in a bit of rice vinegar first), avocado, mayo, yellow radish, cooked leaf spinach. Use 5-8 nori sheets, lay them on a dry work surface, rough side up, and lay strips of the rice and filling down the centre. Roll up tightly tucking it all in and seal the seam with wet fingers. Cut with a very sharp knife to serve.

Edamame: Simmer frozen soybeans in their pods in vegetable stock with some bay leaves, peppercorns, and star anise and maybe allspice for 15 minutes, drain, sprinkle with coarse salt and serve.

Turmeric drink:

1 cup almond or soy milk
1 tsp turmeric powder
½ tsp cinnamon
1 tsp syrup
pepper, cayenne
Grated ginger

Lots of spices have beneficial properties, even in the smallish quantities we tend to consume them in. Turmeric is especially valuable – its anti-inflammatory and anti-oxidant action along with aiding digestion and good sleep makes it a great all rounder for good health in stressful times. Whisk together and gently heat in a pan til warm: almond or soy milk, turmeric powder, cinnamon, sweetener (maple syrup or similar), a pinch of pepper and cayenne or chili, plus a bit of grated ginger (optional).

Nutrition 101

Nutrition is both a simple and a complicated subject. It *should* really be quite easy – humans need nutrients, i.e. particular chemical compounds that do particular things in their bodies such as provide energy or build enzymes, and these can be supplied by all sorts of foods. Although that's indeed what nutrition comes down to, when you start trying to navigate nutrient interactions and effects, and all the (industry-promoted) hype around different health promising-or-supposedly-toxic foods, it gets quite hard to separate fact from fiction. This isn't helped by the effects of industrial agriculture, a profit-seeking food industry, modern stressful lifestyles, a hierarchical and compartmentalised health system, and mass media. We have an exploitative corporate food system, and while our rushed and pressured lives make it hard for us to be healthy, our health system makes it hard for us to effectively or holistically improve our health. The various bits of conflicting and biased information we are given makes it hard for us to understand what exactly are healthy choices. No wonder we are so confused about food.

Understandably, nutrition as a general discipline has become much discredited. Michael Pollan offers an interesting critique of the reductionist basis of nutrition and its exploitation by a food and a health industry[35] – and he's

_____

35 Michael Pollan, *In Defense of Food* – a good read culminating in the advice 'Eat (real) food. Not too much. Mostly plants'.

right, nutrition is full of people selling you their stuff from products to diets to stupid ideas, and you should always take nutritional advice with a large pinch of salt.

Nutrition remains hugely important though, especially considering how much the odds are stacked against most people trying to eat well. It's not easy to find trustworthy information that will work for you and your own individual metabolism (the way your own body, influenced by genetics, your particular enzyme and hormone levels, your activities and gut microbes, uses what you eat). We have too much information – countless websites, nearly 120 000 books searching for 'nutrition' on Amazon, and an army of enthusiastic yet uninformed journalists all telling us what to do, alongside a food industry funding research to tout their products. It's helpful to have a knowledge of the basics and to apply critical thinking skills to nutritional information. Look at the actual evidence for health claims. Look at the credentials of who is saying what. Look for any connections to the food industry and whether someone's trying to sell you something.

Don't take recommendations wholesale. For example, if some study has found that 'strawberries protect against cancer', this is unlikely to mean that you should go and eat strawberries til the cows come home to guarantee immunity. Piecemeal findings of this kind are meaningless out of context. Also it's remarkable what our bodies can do and adapt to. Especially if you are generally fairly healthy, there are few foods (apart from maybe that blowfish dish), that will kill or poison you if you eat it. Fear-mongering or blanket enthusiasm about any single food is usually suspicious. What you want to achieve are some generally healthy and varied eating habits and food choices that feel right and good for you.

Let's start with Basic Nutrition then. Protein, fats and carbohydrates are the **macronutrients**, needed in large amounts in the diet; they provide energy and make up the calorie content of a food. Vitamins and minerals are **micronutrients**, i.e. organic compounds needed in small amounts. You also need water and fibre. However, a pill containing nutrients in proportion wouldn't do the job; it seems you need nutrients in actual foods, and there are ever more other components of foods such as **phytochemicals** that are being discovered to have an effect in our body. The science of exactly how much you need of what may be exact but derived from population averages, and it's unrealistic and undesirable to apply this rigorously to what you eat at an individual level, unless you're on a feeding tube. We all will have more protein one day and less the next, and we will eat cake, and we will eat twice as many calories one day and half the next; that's ok. It's the big picture that matters.

Protein

With backing from the animal industry, the importance of protein in our diets has been subject to misconceptions over the last 70 or so years. We all became convinced that we needed much more protein, and of a certain 'quality' (preferably provided by animal products) than we actually do. Proteins *are* important – they are literally the building blocks of our bodies. They consist of chains of amino acids, of which 8 are 'essential' (i.e. we need to derive them from foods). Your DNA code is just of amino acid combinations; this is how fundamental proteins are.

Proteins from animal flesh are said to be 'first class' or 'complete', as they contain all 8 essential amino acids, and plant derived proteins are said to be 'incomplete'. However, this theory is now a bit old-school as it's been proven time and time again that in a varied plant based diet, you can obtain the 8 necessary amino acids. Protein also doesn't need to be the main focus of our diet, as meat merchants and Atkins dieters would have you believe. A diet containing about 10% of its calories in the form of protein, or 0.8g/per kg bodyweight for someone who isn't intensely exercising, is more than adequate. In fact, many healthy people across the world live on diets of 5% or less.

Our bodies maintain a general pool of amino acids used as building blocks to make things like enzymes. These are then broken down again and fairly efficiently recycled, and the pool only needs a bit of topping up from dietary sources. Excess protein that isn't needed isn't stored or magically turned into muscles, instead it's usually converted to fat to be stored for later use, and the nitrogen that's freed up from the protein is turned into ammonia then urea in the liver and excreted. One of the concerns of high protein diets is that they tax the kidneys and lead to mineral losses due to this process; however evidence isn't too clear around this. Some humans seem to thrive on very high protein and fat diets.

Proteins do have a strong satisfaction factor and make you feel full for longer; and inadequate protein supplies can cause a lot of harm, including affecting your mood through neurotransmitter production.

Good plant protein foods

	Serving size	Grams of protein
Seitan, cooked	100g	21
Soybeans	1 cup cooked	29
Kidney beans	1 cup cooked	15
Black beans	1 cup cooked	42
Peanut butter	1/3 cup	24
Tofu (raw/firm)	½ cup	20
Walnuts	1/2 cup	9
Cooked brown rice	1 cup	5
Wholewheat pasta	1 cup	7.5
Quinoa	1 cup	7.5
Cooked broccoli	1 cup	3.7
Peas	1 cup	8
Chickpeas	1 cup	39
Hempseeds	3 tbsp	10
Soymilk	1 cup	8

Fats

The macronutrients seem to be the main site of disagreement amongst nutrition dogma – how good or bad each one is, and what the best ratio is to have of each. This arguing has really confused things, and especially around fats. We seem to have the idea that eating fats – any fats – directly turns into fat in our bodies, and clogs up our arteries causing heart disease. But neither is true, and fats come in a wide variety and are necessary components of our diet, a good source of energy, and are needed for example for brain development, in our cell membranes and for hormone production. Fat phobia has led to a wide range of low fat products, which involve unnecessary processing, are generally fairly disgusting, often contain compensatory salt or sugar, and mess with your satiety. Fuck the low fat nonsense.

Fats all have the same basic chemical structure, and any food containing fat will have a mixture of different kinds of fatty acid molecules, which break down to individual fatty acids and glycerol (a sugar). There's a lot of talk about which fats are good and bad, so let's try to shed a bit of light on this. There are various distinctions for types of fat:

Saturated or **unsaturated** literally means whether the fatty acid contains all the hydrogen that its carbon atoms can hold, or still have room for 1 hydrogen atom (monounsaturated), or multiple (polyunsaturated). Due to their chemical structure, saturated fats are hard, and unsaturated usually oils. Most fats in meat and dairy are saturated, whereas most plant and fish oils are not (the exceptions being coconut and palm oil).

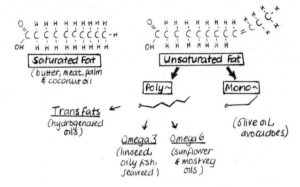

Saturated Fat
(butter, meat, palm & coconut oil)

Unsaturated Fat

Poly~

Mono~

Trans fats (hydrogenated oils)

Omega 3 (linseed, oily fish, seaweed)

Omega 6 (sunflower & most veg oils)

(olive oil, avocados)

Monounsaturated fats are missing one hydrogen atom in their fatty acids, and are considered healthy fats – they occur for example in high ratios in olive oil and avocados.

Polyunsaturated fats are missing multiple hydrogen atoms in their fatty acids, have a kinked structure and are usually plant based and liquid, i.e. an oil. Of these, Omega 3 and 6 fatty acids are the **Essential Fatty Acids**, i.e. we need to get them from our diet. Omega 6 is used for prostaglandins, key in our inflammatory response to injury and stress. It's found in most vegetable oils and is plentiful in our diets – in fact we consume too much. Omega 3 is used for prostacyclins which are anti-inflammatory; they are also necessary for brain development and general mental health – we are still learning about its importance, and as with other nutrients it's being heavily pushed by a supplement industry, so it's hard to trust the hype. It's clear though that our diets today are low in Omega 3. One reason is that we used to obtain it from pastured and wild animals, and with the change to grain feeding, we've lost this source from animal foods.

The most readily available forms of Omega 3 - eicosapentaenoic acid (EPA) and docosahexaenoic acid (DHA) are found in oily fish (e.g. herring, salmon, mackerel, and tuna). With the increased attention Omega 3 is receiving, and a government guideline of eating at least one portion of oily fish a week to help meet needs, there is a clear conflict between improving our Omega 3 levels and the sustainability of our fisheries. Our current oily fish consumption in the UK is at just 1/3 of a portion/week and already threatening ocean biodiversity.

In a plant-based diet, Omega 3's are not that easily obtained though, and something you do need to pay attention to - decent sources that provide the precursors for DHA and EPA are linseeds, some leafy greens, seaweeds and microalgae, hemp seeds and walnuts. Omega 3 oils do not keep well - they go rancid easily and are very light sensitive, which is probably one of the reasons they don't feature much in our shelf-life based food production. Omega 3 oil products are also often just a bit gimmicky and overpriced; you're better off investing in a grinder and making the effort to regularly grind some linseeds (to access the oils) to have in smoothies/on your porridge/force down a spoonful.

Omega 3 and 6 fats compete in the body, meaning the high levels of Omega 6 oils we consume with vegetable oils (especially sunflower) is affecting our use of the little Omega 3 we consume. The ratio in our Western diets is often about 16:1, when it should be much less (exactly how much less is disputed; some even say it needs to be 1:1).

Hydrogenated fats are unsaturated plant oils that have been entirely or partially converted into saturated ones – i.e. turned into hard fats by literally being injected with extra hydrogen atoms. They are used especially in processed foods and commercial baked goods, as they have a long shelf life.

'Trans fats' are hydrogenated or saturated fats that have gone wrong, i.e. they have a particular 'incorrect' molecular arrangement, and are considered especially harmful as they mimic normal fat molecules, but don't fulfill their function. They occur naturally, but are mainly found in partially hydrogenated fats (used for example in commercial pastries or in frying oil).

So, what fats are good and bad? A high intake of saturated fats is said to increase your risk of coronary heart disease by raising 'bad' cholesterol levels, as well as increasing your risk of many types of cancer. Although this has been medical dogma for some time, the evidence around this has always been disputed[36], and saturated fats from different sources have different effects. The main fats to avoid, to

---

36 e.g. Hooper L et al (2015) *Reduction in saturated fat intake for cardiovascular disease*. Cochrane Database Systematic Review

current knowledge, are trans fats, hydrogenated fats, and processed palm oils due to carcinogenic compunds (glycidil fatty acid esters) and rainforest deforestation, and it's worth aiming for a favourable ratio of Omega 3 and 6 fatty acids. A high consumption of oxidised oils – polyunsaturated plant oils that have been damaged e.g. at very high heat, and/or gone rancid – may increase inflammation, cell damage and disease risk, although there is some disagreement about the level of danger. It's probably worth avoiding oils that have gone off, keeping oils stored in cool and dark places, and limiting deep fried foods or re-used oil. In higher cooking temperatures, saturated fats or olive oil are more stable. It's also probably worth getting good quality, non hydrogenated margarine (that's not based on omega 6 heavy sunflower), and only using it sparingly. I know a lot of people who consciously choose butter in place of margarine for taste, ecological and health reasons, but if you prefer to eat vegan, there's also the alternative of simply learning to use less spread.

Most commercial oils are processed, using lots of chemicals and solvents, easily oxidised and may contain trans fats. If you can afford it, an ideal oil collection would include cold pressed (i.e. less processed) extra virgin olive oil, cold pressed rapeseed oil for when you need a more flavourless cooking oil, or sustainably farmed coconut oil as an occasional alternative, and maybe some linseed, sesame, avocado or nut oils for variety in salads and to up your Omega 3 sources.

However, for most of us this needs to be an area of compromise, and straight-up vegetable oil, which in the UK is mainly made from rapeseed, is refined and processed but at least has a decent fatty acid profile with mainly monounsaturated and polyunsaturated fats and a more favourable ratio of Omega 3:Omega 6. If you feel you should supplement, microalgae based Omega 3 pills are available – avoid those that are combined with Omega 6.

Type of oil or fat	Mono %	Saturated %	Poly %	Of which omega 3 %
Coconut	6	86	2	
Butter	21	51	3	
Lard	47	41	12	1
Soybean	26	15	57	7
Olive	76	16	8	
Rapeseed	54	7	37	7
Sesame	42	13	45	
Corn	27	12	54	
Sunflower	20	10	65	
Linseed	19	9	72	58
Avocado	70	20	10	
Hemp	12	8	80	20
Pumpkin	34	9	57	15

http://www.bbc.co.uk/news/magazine-33675975 and Geary (2001) The Food and Mood Handbook.

The exact quantity of fat we should be consuming is not easily quantifed. In most traditional diets, for example in Southeast Asia and India, only about 20% of total calories are supplied by fat, whereas in affluent societies, the figure is more like 40% - mostly from meat and dairy products. However, remember that quality is more important than quantity, and some people do particularly well on a higher fat diet – think about how different fats makes you feel – listening to your body is a good way to gauge how much you should be eating!

Carbohydrates

And another controversial macronutrient; while saturated fats were certainly the villians in the 80s and 90s, the blame for everything has shifted for many to carbs.

MONO-SACCHARIDES

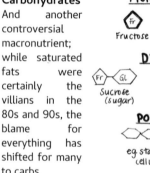

Fructose   Glucose   Galactose

DI-SACCHARIDES

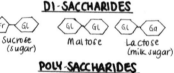

Sucrose (sugar)   Maltose   Lactose (milk sugar)

POLY-SACCHARIDES

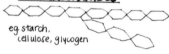

eg. starch, cellulose, glycogen

The basic building block of all carbs are simple sugars, 'monosaccharides'. They can occur in quickly digested pairs ('disaccharides'), or in longer chains of starches ('polysaccharides'), that are broken down to monosaccharides in our digestion. Fibre consists of indigestible polysaccharides.

We have particular associations with carbs, and they do affect our bodies in so many ways:

> blood sugar: emotional resilience, alertness, energy levels, vitality, insulin
> feeding your gut bacteria
> caries and dental health
> intolerances and allergies in some people
> satiety
> cravings
> distinctive tastes and giving foods desirable textures
> feeding our brains, which need a steady supply of glucose (sugar)

Probably their most important role is in maintaining energy levels. The more complex carbs are (longer chained starches/or mixed with fibre), the slower they are digested and used; the simple sugars – sugary and white flour products – are very quickly broken down. Our blood sugar levels are kept in homeostasis, i.e. at a constant level of 3.5-6 mmol/litre. When we eat lots of simple sugars, blood sugar levels swing very high, causing the pancreas to release the hormone insulin. Insulin removes glucose from the blood stream to the muscles or to store it as fat, and brings the blood sugar level back down again. When blood sugar levels are high e.g. after a sugary meal, the body releases a lot of insulin, called an insulin spike, resulting sometimes in a slight overshoot – i.e. too much glucose is removed and blood sugar levels are now too low.

This can lead to the familiar pattern of high energy – crash/low energy/irritability and hunger – quick chocolate bar to still the hunger – and same again!

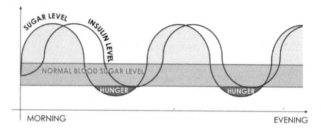

Having a steady, gently undulating, blood sugar level without any major peaks and troughs makes you feel better both longer term and in the short term, affecting mood and emotional resilience, possibly reducing headaches or migraine in some people, as well as period pain.

Insulin resistance occurs when cells don't respond as readily to insulin action, i.e. don't take up glucose from the blood meaning the body needs to produce more insulin to get blood sugar levels down. The problem is that insulin also has other effects in the body, both hormonal and direct, e.g. stimulating fat cells to store fats, affecting blood pressure and heart health, affecting use of proteins and more, and that insulin resistance may be a precursor to diabetes. Its development is linked to genetic susceptibility, stress which inhibits the effects of insulin, low levels of physical activity, and regular high levels of insulin or insulin spikes and troughs.

Is sugar... evil??

We've evolved with a sweet tooth – sweet things provide us with easily digested instant energy – but we are eating so much more sugar than at any point in history, and it's right to be suspicious of the effects this might have on our metabolism, hormones, and long term health.

The list of concerns around sugar include:
- ➢ empty calories, i.e. energy without any actual nutrients
- ➢ dental health and caries
- ➢ promoting inflammation
- ➢ high blood sugar and insulin resistance – links to diabetes, heart disease, and cancers
- ➢ promoting overeating by not signaling satiety
- ➢ glycation – sugar reacting with proteins in your body creating 'advanced glycation end products', associated with aging, heart disease and Alzheimers
- ➢ being addictive due to dopamine rewards

Sugar is a disaccharide consisting of glucose and fructose. The latter follows a different metabolic process to glucose – larger amounts need to metabolised in the liver where they're converted to fat, and they may contribute to insulin resistance. High fructose corn syrup (HFCS) – thankfully not very common in the UK but a major ingredient in the

US – exacerbates all the above[37]. It was developed after the Cuban missile crisis affected the supply of sugar in the US, and contains a 55/45% fructose to glucose ratio.

Sugar refining is an intense chemical process potentially involving bone char from animals and a lot of chemicals (brown sugar is sometimes just refined sugar that has then had molasses added back to it – raw sugar on the other hand has actually had slightly less processing).

Sugars aren't necessarily 'pure white and deadly' as John Yudkin's influential book from 1972 first proposed, but they may be affecting your health and are ubiquituos. Read through any extensive ingredients list and you'll find chemical terms ending in -ose which are all different types of sugars. It's worth trying to cut down – this could be replacing sugary drinks with water, not snacking on sugary snacks all the time, or leaving the sugar out of your coffee. Your tastebuds will quickly adjust.

Are artificial sweeteners... evil??
Sweeteners such as saccharin, sucralose, and aspartame were developed in labs and there's been much concern

---

37 Fructose when consumed with fibres, e.g. naturally occurring in fruit, is not much of a problem, it's the large amounts that are. Agave syrup, promoted as a healthy sugar alternative, is made up of 80% fructose!

over their potential effects, but long term and conclusive studies are still lacking. They do trick your taste buds, dulling their sweet response and messing with your blood sugar levels and insulin response, as well as offering zero satisfaction.

Is gluten... evil??

Gluten is a protein found in wheat, rye, oats (in lower amounts) and barley. An estimated 1% people are allergic (celiac disease), where an immune reaction damages the intestinal wall. You can be tested for celiac disease with a simple blood test. Some – it's impossible to know how many exactly – are intolerant, i.e. gluten can cause digestive problems, bloating, and discomfort. There is little knowledge as yet of the long term effects of gluten intolerance.

Although wheat is the defining grain of thousands of years of Western civilisation, in recent years its quality has declined due to intensive farming and industrial refining, and we have been eating more and more of it, leading to an increase in related illnesses and intolerances. Some may benefit from reducing gluten, varying their diet more, or cutting it out altogether. Not everyone is equally affected though, so if you seem fine with it, there's not much point denying yourself tasty pie for no reason. And bear in mind that many gluten free products are processed foods with a lot of salt, fats, sugar, and additives.

Is soy... evil?

Soya certainly has health benefits, and is a good source of fibre and protein. However, it also contains phytates, which influence our absorption of minerals, and oestrogen like substances called isoflavones that are said on the one hand to lower 'bad' cholesterol and relieve menopausal symptoms while on the other, to affect female cycles and male fertility. Concerns are mostly exaggerated, and it is hard to separate fact from fiction when it comes to soy, as both the anti-soy and the pro-soy lobbies are hugely vocal. Soya can also affect iodine levels and therefore thyroid function and metabolism. The fermentation of soybeans lessens this iodine depletion, so products such as tamari, miso and tempeh are exceptions.

Like anything (apart from green leafy vegetables maybe), soya in excess is probably not good for you. One of the things that people often do when they adopt a vegan diet is replace all meat and dairy products with soy products, which does not make for a balanced diet. Organic is preferable to non organic, as soy is often excessively sprayed with pesticides, grown in monocultures responsible for deforestation, or could be genetically modified. However, the majority of the soy harvest in the world is fed to animals with the byproducts used in vegetable oils, often hydrogenated and used in processed foods.

Fibre
Fibre is the indigestible part of plant foods. It can either be:
Soluble – in oats, lentils, fruit, and some vegetables. This type of fibre is more gel like and slows down digestion and stomach emptying. It's fermented by bacteria in the gut to short chain fatty acids, which are good for the immune

system, lower LDL ('bad') cholesterol, and make vitamins. Soluble fibre also improves insulin sensitivity as it delays glucose absorption.

Insoluble - in wholegrains and vegetables. It absorbs water, adds bulk, and prevents constipation by speeding up passage through the intestine.

The daily recommendation for intakes is 18g fibre/day in the UK, but this is just a guideline. Some people struggle with too much fibre, especially those with bowel issues and Irritable Bowel Syndrome, and may do better with the soluble rather than insoluble type.

If you usually have a lot of fibre, it's worth making sure you are also keeping well hydrated as it holds water. Although it doesn't provide nutrients directly, fibre's a very important part of our diet (as anyone who is low on fibre and constipated would attest), also due to its role in supporting gut bacteria. If you don't usually have much fibre, increase it gradually, rather than upping it suddenly – your gut won't know what's hit it!

Glycemic Index (GI)
The GI describes how quickly a carbohydrate is digested and enters the bloodstream. It's influenced by fibre content, length of the carbon chain carbohydrate molecule, sugar composition, physical structure, and other factors. It varies and is not really a very reliable measure, but can give you a bit of an idea of how a food will affect your blood sugar and energy levels.

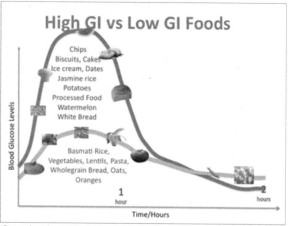

High GI vs Low GI Foods

Blood Glucose Levels

Chips
Biscuits, Cakes
Ice cream, Dates
Jasmine rice
Potatoes
Processed Food
Watermelon
White Bread

Basmati Rice,
Vegetables, Lentils, Pasta,
Wholegrain Bread, Oats,
Oranges

1
hour

2
hours

Time/Hours

So, it's clear that the slow release of carb energy and avoiding insulin spikes is desirable both for your short term mood and energy levels and for your long term health. Things you can do to help achieve this include: more low GI and fibrous foods, less simple sugars and sugars and refined carbs, eating protein and some fats (which helps slow digestion), considering whether you feel better eating smaller portions but more frequently or full meals with greater gaps, and not skipping meals. Caffeine, nicotine, and even alcohol (though it's not a stimulant) all cause our blood sugar to rise due to a spike in adrenaline and cortisol. Remember how stress and cortisol production inhibits insulin? Exercise – even just walking – also helps regulate insulin. Finally, get enough sleep - sleep deprivation also has a dramatic effect on blood sugar and insulin levels.

If you're worried about diabetes or potential insulin resistance, it's a fairly simple procedure at your GP's to get your blood sugar tested.

Food and Mood Diaries

If you have varying moods and energy levels, or you're wondering whether you might be sensitive to caffeine/sugar/refined carbs, or would like to identify what your daily habits actually look like, it's worth trying to keep a food diary for a couple of days. Keeping a diary is just for yourself, to help you identify patterns rather than be scrutinised by others or judge yourself from. If the idea makes you feel at all uneasy or anxious, don't do it. There's nothing to gain from obsessing or worrying about what you eat.

For a period of 1-3 days, carry a small notebook with you and write down everything you eat and drink. You don't need to measure everything, a rough description is enough. Try to include water as well, and a note on physical activity or unusual occurrences during the day. You can also include some notes on your sleep.

Then include how you felt while eating each snack or meal, and if you notice symptoms or changes, also in the 1-2 hours after eating. You can rate symptoms from 1 (low) to 5 (high). A sample layout is included below:

Time & date	Food/ drink	How I feel physically	How I feel emotionally	Physical activity	Other notes
Mon/ 12th					
8am	Coffee (black, 2 sugars)	Tired (3), aching (4)			
8.30	Bowl of porridge with golden syrup	Tired (2)			
9am				Walk to work, 15 mins	
10am	Coffee (black, 2 sugars)	Ok	Alert (3), calm (2)		
10.40			Anxious (2)		
...					
0.15 – 7am	Sleep: fell asleep quickly but then woke a few times through the night				

Food and mood diary analysis:

Can you identify any eating styles? Are there large gaps between meals and snacks or do you graze?

Is your diet varied? What types of foods do you usually eat and how much/often? (sweet, starchy carbs, protein foods, fibre-containing foods, fatty foods, alcohol, coffee, tea, cola, foods containing additives)

Do you skip meals? Are you eating patterns chaotic?

Do you eat at roughly the same time each day?

Where do you anguish over food?

Are you aware when eating?

What emotional states or situations trigger cravings?

Are you an emotional eater?

Any prime suspects for effects? (I.e. noticeably feeling better or worse within an hour of eating/drinking something).

When and how do you feel like you may have overeaten and can you identify any potential reasons for this?

How do you feel in the couple hours after caffeine, sugars, high protein meals?

Water

is essential to life, and essential in your diet. It makes up about 60% of our body weight and we need plenty every day. Symptoms of dehydration include headaches, dizziness, dark urine, sluggishness, constipation, and being well hydrated helps cognitive and physical performance, maintain body temperature, and decreases the risk of infection and heart disease. Drink your water! A general guideline is 8 (medium size) glasses a day but you might need more or less depending on activity levels, your diet etc. E.g. if you drink lots of coffee or alcohol, which are both diuretic and make you wee more, you should compensate with some extra water.

Micronutrients

is the term for vitamins and minerals, which are compounds found in our foods and needed by our bodies for a whole range of functions – from building our bones  to facilitating energy production to making hormones. The best way to obtain enough vitamins and minerals is by a eating a good variety of foods, especially whole foods.

Dietary Recommended Values (DRVs) are what's considered the average amount an individual needs daily of a given nutrient. There's always other things that might be interfering with your micronutrient nutrition though – e.g. eating 20g of iron listed on a packet doesn't mean your body now has 20g of iron; the absorption – i.e. what's actually made available to the body and not just excreted – can vary greatly. This can be due to other factors in food, cooking, or your own body's metabolism. Your micro-nutrient levels can also be depleted by factors such as high alcohol or sugar intakes, stress, too much fibre or oxalic acid inhibiting mineral absorption, or unbalanced intakes.

If you suspect you are deficient in something, don't just randomly supplement, but seek medical advice and do your research before deciding on a supplement regime. General multivitamins and mineral supplements, though they sound like they can't do harm, have not been shown to produce any benefit in long term studies, and too much of certain micronutrients or an imbalance can do harm. If you feel better from taking a multivitamin or a nutrition supplement, one with low dosages or a preparation such as Floradix (mainly iron and B vitamins) may be of more benefit.

VITAMINS are compounds essential to digestion, energy metabolism, and many other body processes. The following pages are not exhaustive, and only list a few interesting functions, deficiency symptoms, and highlight the main plant based sources.

FAT SOLUBLE
can be stored so not needed daily, and toxic in high doses

Vitamin A and its precursors in plants, carotenoids, e.g. beta-carotene. Enhances immunity, skin and eyes, antioxidant Deficiencies: dry hair/skin, dry eyes, night blindness Sources: dark leafy greens, red and yellow fruit and veg e.g. carrots, sweet potatoes, squash, mangos

Vitamin D Growth, bone health, immunity (e.g. colds and flu in winter) Deficiencies: low levels common, rickets, brittle bones, muscle weakness Sources: mainly from the sun, in the Northern hemisphere only between March-Oct 15 mins/day of exposed skin (without sunscreen, longer for darker skin and the elderly) usually sufficient to build up stores. Very few plant sources e.g. fortified foods, mushrooms, nettles and sweet potatoes.

Vitamin E Antioxidant. Destroyed by high heat
Deficiencies: often low levels but deficiencies rare. Leg cramps
Sources: avocados, cold pressed veg oil, dark leafy greens

Vitamin K Mostly synthesised by gut bacteria and affected by antibiotics or low fibre intakes. Blood clotting and bone health
Sources: green leafy veg, parsley, fermented foods

WATER SOLUBLE
needed more frequently, lost in cooking water or through exposure

Vitamin C (ascorbic acid) Lots of functions including anti stress and immune system. Antioxidant. Increases absorption from plant iron. Levels reduced by alcohol, antidepressants, steroids and smoking.
Deficiencies: bleeding gums, low immunity, slow wound healing
Sources: citrus fruit, berries, green veg, sweet potatoes, red peppers, kiwis and mango

Vitamin B1 (thiamine) Brain function, antioxidant. Affected by antibiotics, alcohol or caffeine. Need increased in a high carb diet
Deficiencies: beriberi, constipation, edema
Sources: whole grains, pulses and soymilk, brown rice

Vitamin B2 (riboflavin) Antibody production, skin, nails and hair
Deficiencies: cracks/sores around the mouth, skin lesions
Sources: legumes, whole grains, spinach, dark leafy greens, mushrooms

Vitamin B3 (niacin) Circulation, memory and nervous system, healthy skin. Need increased in strenuous exercise. Affected by alcohol and antibiotics
Deficiencies: Pellagra
Sources: mushrooms, leafy green veg, peanut butter, tofu, potatoes
Can also be made from the protein tryptophan

Vitamin B5 (panthothenic acid) Antistress – adrenal hormones, neurotransmitters.
Deficiencies: rare - fatigue, headaches, tingling in hands
Sources: avocados, legumes, mushrooms, nuts, whole grains, potatoes, broccoli

Vitamin B6 (pyridoxine) Anti-cancer and heart disease, cognitive performance, helps B12 and essential fatty acid use, good for PMS. Need increased with antidepressants and oral contraceptives
Deficiencies: anemia, headaches, flaky skin, sore tongue, depression
Sources: bananas, watermelon, avocado, potatoes, brewers yeast, carrots, peas, spinach, sunflower seeds, walnuts, wheat germ

> **Vitamin B12** (cobalmin) Nervous system, converts homocysteine. Deficiencies are serious and can be masked by folic acid, so caution is advised, and it's only available in animal foods or fortified foods (yeast extract, plant milks)
>
> Supplement: 10mcg/day or 2000mcg 1x week

*Plus **Biotin** – for hair and skin and fat metabolism – **Choline** for brain function and heart health – **Folate** for brain function and immunity and important in early pregnancy*

Homocysteine is formed in the breakdown of methionine (especially from animal products), and high levels have been said to interfere with neurotransmitter production (e.g. serotonin), and linked to inflammation and increased risk of heart disease. B12 is necessary for homocysteine conversion and low B12 in vegetarians and vegans has been shown to result in high homocysteine levels[38].

Antioxidants counter the negative effects of cell damaging free radicals, which are unstable molecules formed naturally but also from pollution and irritants.

MINERALS are inorganic nutrients and trace metals we need. They are often interdependent or compete with each other for absorption or use, e.g. too much zinc depletes

---

38 Obersby et al (2013) *Plasma total homocysteine status of vegetarians compared with omnivores: a systematic review and meta-analysis.* British Journal of Nutrition, Jan 8

copper, or high levels of calcium affects magnesium – so seek advice if supplementing.

Calcium Bones and teeth, heartbeat and nerves, helps protect against cancer and heart disease. Needs Vitamin D and the amino acid lysine for absorption. Inhibited by iron and zinc and also depleted by sugar, stress, coffee, alcohol and high salt intakes.

It's not just calcium but also vitamin D, magnesium and other micronutrients along with weight bearing exercise, not smoking, higher body weight, and low sodium, caffeine and alcohol intakes all all lower the risk of developing osteoporosis (brittle bones). Calcium isn't particularly better or worse from dairy compared to plant sources.

Deficiencies: brittle nails and white spots, eczema, numbness, insomnia, muscle cramps

Sources: dark green veg, molasses, bok choy, almonds, tofu/soy, pulses, oranges

Iron Blood. Haem-iron from animals is better absorbed than plant based iron. Absorption of plant iron increased by Vitamin C, and decreased by combination with tea/tannins and phytic acid in fibre.

Deficiencies: The most common deficiency. Impaired immune system, tiredness, brittle hair, poor mental development.

Sources: pulses, nuts, dried fruit, whole grains, dark green leafy veg, peas, potatoes

Magnesium Nerve transmission, heart function, muscle contraction, teeth and bones. Helps with PMS and fatty acid metabolism.
Deficiencies: Common due to low levels in soil and poor absorption, but full blown deficiencies are rare. Muscle cramps, anxiety and insomnia, irregular heartbeat, chocolate cravings
Sources: dark chocolate/cocoa, pumpkin seeds, pulses, nuts esp. cashews, dark leafy greens, oats, millet, potatoes

Sodium i.e. salt (sodium chloride) Fluid balance, nervous system signaling, adrenal glands. Needed in balance with potassium.

Potassium Nervous system, fluid balance, heart rhythm, blood pressure. Need increased from stress, absorption affected by tobacco and caffeine.
Deficiencies: Can be caused by losses through dehydration, and some medications and steroids. Dry skin, thirst, depression
Sources: potato, sweet potato, broccoli and spinach, carrots, banana, avocado, pulses, soybeans

Phosphorus In many foods so deficiencies rare, but too much phosphorus (especially from carbonated drinks) can cause calcium loss and cravings for sugar and alcohol.

Iodine Thyroid function and hormones. Not many plant sources so fortified foods and sea vegetables are

important. Too much isn't good either though
Deficiencies: muscle cramps, cold hands and feet, poor memory, goitre
Sources: seafoods, iodised salt, dark green vegetables (levels vary greatly though)

Selenium Antioxidant, immune system. Soil concentrations decreasing
Sources: brazil nuts, cabbage, courgettes, seeds, whole grains

Chromium Important for blood sugar regulation (enhances insulin), and deficiency is common.
Sources: molasses, nuts, whole grains, potatoes, pears, broccoli

Zinc Mental development and mental health, blood sugar, fatty acid metabolism, injury prevention, tissue healing and immune system. Need increased in stress
Deficiencies: Often low levels. Hair loss, lesions, impaired immune response
Sources: pulses and lentils, seeds, nuts, whole grains, root vegetables, leafy veg

Also: Chromium - Sulphur - Boron - Cobalt - Copper - Manganese - Molybdenum - Silicon - Vanadium

Salt is a molecule made up of sodium and chloride, and it's often said that we are eating too much. The main concern has been over its links to hypertension, i.e. high blood pressure causing damage to blood vessels and increasing the risk of heart disease. However, only an estimated 25% of the population is actually sensitive to the long term effect of salt on blood pressure, and the response in individual blood pressure varies widely from dietary interventions[39]. The dietary recommendation to watch salt intakes – especially from processed foods – remains relevant though, since high salt intakes can still affect kidneys, fluid retention leading to bloating etc, calcium levels, and increase the risk of cognitive decline. Sodium is needed in a balance with potassium (i.e. a high salt intake will require more potassium), and processed foods in particular often have a unfavourable ratio.

There's also much controversy around the quality of salt. It should really be fairly straightforward, as salt all has the same origin and basic chemical composition. It's from the sea or mined, and either stripped of extra elements (both toxic and beneficial) leaving just the sodium chloride, or  left with some trace elements (often causing a slight discolouring), and either ground or left in rock crystals.

There's been criticisms of high levels of heavy metals in rock salts, but in the end you don't (or shouldn't) eat much of it anyway. Himalayan pink salt is tasty but a bit

---

39 There is also a strong correlation between hypertension and race or class, as mentioned in the chapter on the social determinants of health.

overhyped, and as an imported product we should probably be wary about the impact of Western enthusiasm for it. Table salt is more likely to have iodine added – a beneficial addition as iodine food sources are rare – and (harmless) anti caking agents, and sea salt more likely to have extra trace minerals (but in negligible amounts), may be slightly less processed, and does often have a better flavour. The jury's out exactly what difference this all might make nutritionally though.

'**Antinutrients**' is a term given to substances in plant foods that interfere with nutrient use, e.g. inhibit mineral absorption, or leech vitamins, or are toxic in some way or the other, often as a chemical defense for the plants. Examples include saponins, phytates, and enzyme inhibitors. However their effects are often lessened by processing, e.g. soaking, germinating, cooking. They may even also have beneficial effects in the body. Generally, antinutrients are found in otherwise healthy foods whose benefits outweigh negative effects, so in most cases and in a balanced diet they shouldn't be cause for too much concern.

Digestive System
It's really helpful to understand how your digestive system works to get an idea of how your body uses your food, and what kinds of things could be going wrong. Digestive discomforts from bloating to problems pooing are very common after all.

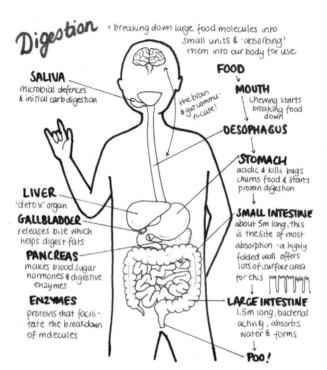

Digestion
= breaking down large food molecules into small units & 'absorbing' them into our body for use

SALIVA
microbial defences & initial carb digestion

the brain & gut communicate!

FOOD

MOUTH
chewing starts breaking food down

OESOPHAGUS

STOMACH
acidic & kills bugs chums food & starts protein digestion

LIVER
'detox' organ

GALLBLADDER
releases bile which helps digest fats

PANCREAS
makes blood sugar hormones & digestive enzymes

ENZYMES
proteins that facilitate the breakdown of molecules

SMALL INTESTINE
about 5m long, this is the site of most absorption - a highly folded wall offers lots of surface area for this

LARGE INTESTINE
1.5m long, bacterial activity, absorbs water & forms

POO!

Our gut is literally a tube spanning mouth to anus, through which we take in food, break it down both mechanically and chemically from large molecules (e.g. the long chain starches) into small units (e.g. monosaccharides) to be absorbed into our bodies, and then eliminate the rest. The diagram shows this 'passage' of food in a finely tuned process coordinated by hormones and feedback systems.

An area of new research and many exciting developments is around the **microbiota** – bacteria and yeasts that colonise our guts. It's estimated we have about 100 trillion microorganisms inhabiting our body, with most of them in our gut and particularly our large intestine (about 2kg worth!). We're born sterile, but immediately start being colonised through friendly bacteria passed on in our mums' birth canal and her breast milk, then further through the environment and diet. By the time we are 3, our microbiome should have established itself, but will continually be affected by what we eat and do, including infections, parasites, and antibiotics.

Although research into this area is quite young, it's clear that a healthy gut has a flourishing, diverse microbiome. Only a tiny fraction of microorganisms are harmful to us, and these can be crowded out by the 'friendly' bacteria inhabiting our gut, one of the many ways they contribute to our immune defence. They also help break down nutrients and produce others such as Vitamin K or biotin, break down toxins, affect our metabolism and use of nutrients, and even affect our mental health, stress hormone levels, and behaviours. There is a strong connection between the brain and gut that we still have much to learn about[40].

A less healthy microbiome might have not recovered after antibiotic use or a parasite infection, or be affected by an

---

40 There's lots of disturbing animal experiments involving influencing the microbiota to then observe behaviours, including purposefully bred 'germ free mice'. We could really do with better research here.

unhealthy diet – bacteria feed and thrive on specific foods, e.g. fibre, and a junk food white-flour-fried foods-processed meats diet has been known to reduce diversity[41].

Digestive disorders are common, and for example IBS (Irritable Bowel Syndrome) affects 10-20% of the population in developed countries, and although exact causes are still undefined, it's often characterised by low levels of microbial activity in the gut.

The market for **probiotic** products such as supplements or probiotic yoghurts or drinks is growing. Keep in mind though that foods with real 'live' bacteria don't suit supermarket shelves (see the following chapter on fermented foods to find out how they're best made at home). There's also little evidence of consistent effects for probiotic supplementation, though this doesn't mean they are worth trying, in particular cases. Not to be confused with **prebiotics,** which are particular compounds in food that our good bacteria thrive on, such as inulin, GOS (galacto-oligo-saccharides) and beta-glucans. These are found in leeks, onions, jerusalem and globe artichokes, garlic, asparagus, and chicory, with higher levels when eaten raw. Another prebiotic is resistant starch, developed when you cook potatoes or rice and then cool it down, e.g. for potato salad or sushi.

---

41 Tim Spector (2015) *The Diet Myth*.

FODMAPS

is short for Fermentable Oligo-, Di-, Mono-saccharides and Polyols, which are short chain carbs that aren't always easily absorbed and so end up being fermented in your large intestine, potentially causing bloating and digestive discomfort. They aren't bad for you at all, and shouldn't be a problem for most people, but if you struggle with digestive discomfort or IBS symptoms it could be a useful strategy to try to reduce them. The diet is very restrictive – you cut down on a large amount of foods including wheat, barley and rye, garlic, onion, most fruit, many veg including brassicas, leeks and mushrooms, beans and pulses, certain sweeteners, dairy, and some drinks including camomile tea. After a few weeks you could then start reintroducing individual foods to see how they affect you and whether you need to keep them out of your diet longer term. It's not recommended to embark on a low FODMAP diet, or easy to find full guidelines without the support of a doctor or dietitian however.

General tips for a healthy digestion:
➤ Eat slowly, with less distraction, and chew well
➤ Pay attention to your internal hunger and satiety signals and the patterns of eating that work well for you
➤ Eat a variety of fruit and veg including prebiotics, and enough fibre
➤ Drink plenty of water
➤ Try to identify foods you might be sensitive to
➤ Don't take antibiotics unnecessarily (including potentially via industrially farmed animal food!), and if you

do need to, take the full course, and help your gut repopulate after, with acidophilus and/or live foods and prebiotics

➤ Reduce sugars (to improve your microbiome diversity) and alcohol (to avoid intestinal permeability and potential leaky gut)

➤ Include 'live' fermented foods in your diet

➤ Practise methods of reducing or coping with stress

Eat Food

So, out of all this information, what's relevant to you? There is no one perfect diet that is healthy and sustainable, so there's not much point searching for it. Instead, learn to listen to your body, figuring out what kind of foods, what kind of eating style, what kinds of cooking suit you.

Some good ideas for healthy eating:

➤ The less processed food the better

➤ Avoiding or eating fewer inflammatory foods where possible – especially if you suffer from inflammatory conditions (trans fats, sugar and sugary drinks, white bread, fried foods, too much omega 6 and margarines, dairy if you are lactose intolerant and gluten if you are gluten intolerant, processed meat and grain fed animals, too much alcohol, artificial food additives)

➤ Including anti inflammatory foods such as turmeric, seaweeds and berries, and healthy fats such as extra virgin olive oil and a source of omega 3s

➤ Drinking more water and less sugary drinks

➤ Including foods good for gut health e.g. prebiotics, and fermented foods

➢ And most importantly, a good variety of vegetables and some fruit, ideally local/fresh/in season – eat the rainbow!

It's not worth obsessing over food[42]. If you are worried about 'toxins', take heart in the fact that we have a really good natural detox system in our liver and kidneys – eat to support them[43]. Be wary of unbalanced eating – from juice detox diets to never eating any vegetables to replacing every bit of dairy with soy products to just eating slabs of meat, one sided diets can do harm. Our bodies generally do best when we give them a nice variety of foods, and when we do, no foods are really 'bad'.

If you are suffering from any particular condition, mental or physical or just feeling under the weather, it's worth looking at dietary changes you can make and gauging if there's any improvement, such as avoiding gluten for digestive issues or focusing on low glycemic index carbs, checking your micronutrient intakes, cutting down on refined sugar, caffeine or other stimulants for your mental health, upping fruit and veg intakes and diversity and supporting your immune system if you are having treatment.

.

----

42 Orthorexia is a form of disordered eating expressing itself as an anxiety over eating only the right, healthy foods.
43 Also a quick note here on organic foods – it's now become a label that just means no chemical pesticides were used and someone could afford certification, but doesn't tell you much else about about the quality of the food or how it's been produced.

'Superfoods' is what usually quite obscure natural products that make for a easy to market commodity are called, usually nicked from some indigenous culture and sold as a panacea for all our Western health woes. They can be a nice treat and an interesting way to vary your diet (and I really like the malty taste of maca, for example) but not necessarily worth their cost or their potentially exploitative practises.

There are plenty of good and more easily come by plant foods that are worth trying to enjoy regularly in your diet for their nutrient density and for particular beneficial phytochemicals (which we are still in the process of learning about and understanding!).

Green leafy veg especially kale and spinach – with a host of micronutrients including iron and calcium and the anti-inflammatory bioflavonoid quercetin - should really play a significant role in plant nutrition. Just one extra serving a day has been associated with lower incidence of diabetes, heart disease and hip fractures.

Seaweed – one of our few plant sources of iodine, adding seaweeds to your cooking is exciting and worthwhile. Full of vitamins, minerals, antioxidants and fibre, some omega 3 fatty acids and helpful for digestive health, though it shouldn't be overeaten either.

Berries – rich in vitamins and phytochemicals with beneficial properties (antioxidant, supporting immune system, reducing heart disease risk, improving brain function).

Avocados – a great source of vitamins (including the obscure K), potassium, fibre, monounsaturated fat, and antioxidants, not to mention creamy deliciousness[44].

Garlic and ginger – both have a range of active phytochemicals, improving bloodflow and reducing clotting, and with anti-inflammatory action. Garlic is also anti-cancer, helps maintain healthy cholesterol levels, and helps the immune system with powerful antibacterial, antiviral and anti-fungal activity. Ginger is an antioxidant, a cough suppressant, good for nausea and motion sickness, stimulates circulation, and anti-spasmodic (e.g. good for menstrual pain).

Pumpkin and pumpkin seeds – high in zinc, soluble fibres, vitamin A and other antioxidants, and the seeds are also high in tryptophan (the protein which is a precursor for serotonin), selenium and iron.

Sweet potatoes – especially the delicious orange fleshed versatile and sweet root vegetables have high levels of nutrients from vitamin C and D, potassium, iron, magnesium and carotenoids, and are prebiotic (supporting your good gut bacteria) too.

Cinnamon and turmeric – the most potent anti-inflammatory and antioxidant spices (and tasty too).

---

44 As with many imported foods experiencing a fad interest (see quinoa!) increased avocado demand is causing deforestation and pollution e.g. in Mexico (The Independent, 2016)

Mushrooms especially shii-take, and wild ones like porcini – good levels of selenium and other antioxidants, B and D vitamins, plus beta-glucans fibre which activates the immune system.

Nettle – high levels of minerals, vitamins (especially iron and vitamin C), anti-inflammatory properties, diuretic and kidney supporting, and best of all free!

Further reading:
Linda Bacon (2010) Eat Well
Guilia Enders ((2014) Gut
Stephen Walsh (2003) Plant Based Nutrition and Health
Marion Nestle (2006) What to Eat

------------------**RECIPES: FERMENTED FOODS**------------------

Fermenting foods, i.e. making use of microorganisms to convert carbohydrates to alcohol or acids, either to make tasty delicious booze, or to make foods easier to digest, more nutritious, or easier to keep (e.g. cheese, olives, yoghurt) is a practise with a long history. With the knowledge we are gaining about the importance of microbial diversity in our gut, we've also been rediscovering the benefits particularly of sour lacto-fermentation of foods such as sauerkraut or kimchi. Behind the hype Is a very traditional and very worthwhile expansion to your palate that will do most digestives systems good too. Fermented foods with 'live' cultures are rare and expensive to buy, so the best way to get them in your diet is making them yourself. Some of the easiest things you can make at home are krauts, kimchi and tonics such as kombucha or kefir.

Guidelines for fermenting projects

➤ Use clean (but not sterilised), ideally wide mouthed, non-metallic jars. I usually wash well, then rinse through with boiling water before filling.

➤ Chop/shred veg finely, then massage. Use your hands. Work the salt in.

➤ Use de-chlorinated water (chlorine kills microorganisms) – either leave tap water to stand a couple of days before using or boil it so it can evaporate, or filter it.

➤ Avoid metal for your cultures such as kefir grains, use plastic spoons.

➤ Allow air to escape your ferments, either with an airlock or by using a kilner jar (avoid tightly screwing lids). Keep the outside air *out* by making sure it's covered in liquids.

➤ Consider the temperature. Medium warm is best for most ferments but follow guidelines if there are any. Keep out of the sun.

➤ The more salt you use, the slower the fermentation and the sourer the result. Too much salt can kill the whole thing.

➢ If your ferment develops mould, chuck it. It's just a fact of fermenting that it can go wrong. This is part of what makes it exciting.

Water kefir: The white 'grains' that are the basis of kefir are colonies of over 30 yeasts and bacteria that multiply fairly easily and have been passed down over many generations. They're traditionally used in milk to make a sour drink but you can also make water kefir (or you can try it in other liquids such as coconut water). Water kefir, fermented with a bit of lemon and raisins to add flavour, is a refreshing, very lightly alcoholic drink.

The grains need regular care and feeding with sugars but I quite enjoy the rhythm of making a new batch every few days. It's good to remove the grains as they multiply – the best thing is to pass them on, and that's the main way you will get any grains to start a culture with!

Sauerkraut: You can literally 'kraut' any vegetables – the basic recipe involves white cabbage. Finely slice, then massage it in a bowl with salt (about 50g to 2kg cabbage). Mix, then press – really pack down - into a clean wide mouthed container; this should release some liquid. Cover the kraut with a plate or something that fits inside the opening, and weight this down to keep it all submerged. A brine should form and rise above the cover within a day (if it doesn't, add a bit of salt water).

Check often – remove any scum and rinse the plate, and check the taste after a week and again after 10 days. When it's softened and sour tasting, it's ready!

Kimchi (fills a 2.5 litre jar or a few smaller ones):

1 large Chinese cabbage (about 1.2 kg)
100g coarse sea salt (less if you are using table salt)
1 litre water
4 spring onions
1.5 cm piece of root ginger
3 cloves of garlic
1 small mooli/daikon/white radish (about 400g)
dark soy sauce or toasted sesame oil (optional)
4 tbsp Korean chilli powder, or cayenne and paprika mixed
1 tbsp sugar

This is my Korean mum's kimchi recipe. Cut off any discoloured bits of the cabbage, then quarter lengthways and cut quarters into 5cm long pieces if you like. Mix the cabbage in a large bowl with most of the salt and some water, rubbing salt into the root ends of the cabbage as you submerge it. Cover the bowl with a plate with a weight on it and put aside in a cool place for 6-12 hours. You are aiming to soften and wilt the cabbage; it should be bendy at the end of the process. Drain, keeping the water, and rinse well a few times. Peel and julienne slice the white radish (into thin strips) and mix it in a small bowl with some soy sauce or sesame oil (optional) and 1 tbsp chilli pepper, massaging it all in well. Finely chop the spring onions and mix in with the radish.

Peel and finely chop the garlic and the ginger. Mix this in a bowl with the drained cabbage along with the rest of the chilli and sugar. Add the radish mixture stuffing it between the leaves. Stuff this into clean, dry jars leaving a good gap at the top, and pour in enough of the salted soaking water to just about cover (not too much). Cover the jar loosely with a lid, and set aside in a cool place to ferment for 1-7 days. Sniff to check – it should get a bit sour, but not too strong. Keep in the fridge for a few more days before eating. It will keep in a cool dark place for quite a long time.

Further Reading:
Sandor Ellis Katz (2016) Wild Fermentation

The Anti-Vegetarian Myth or Reclaiming Veganism

Personally, I'm an advocate of plant foods and that should be pretty clear from what I've been writing here so far. There are many reasons to be vegan. It *should* be fairly straightforward – our food system is terrible and rife with animal cruelty, and if you care at all about that, don't eat animal products. And very few would disagree that our current treatment of animals is wrong and cruel, and that for ecological reasons at least we should work towards abolishing animal factory farming and reducing our total consumption of animal products significantly. Then why is it so difficult and often so very emotive? Why do we have a very polarised debate with people passionately defending their meat eating or trying to prove that humans are evolutionary herbivores or whole websites devoted to helping you cope with vegan arguments? Why are there so many ex-vegans who've crumbled at the lure of triple cheese pizza and now eat anything and everything with no apparent shame? Why are there so many jokes about annoying vegans, foodies scoffing at margarine and soymilk, and anarchists writing extensive critiques of vegetarianism and veganism[45]?

There has been a lot of constructive criticism making some very valid points, e.g. difficulties around single issue politics, the importance of an intersectional veganism i.e. an understanding that connects various oppressions, including feminism and anti-racism, or the illusion of cruelty free consumption[46]. Some criticisms are less about veganism as such and probably more about vegan individuals. Vegan and/or animal rights culture, with a visible tendency to be self-celebratory, preachy, consumerist, white and middle class dominated and sometimes surprisingly oblivious to social and political context (PETA campaigns, anyone?), can unfortunately really be a bit off putting.

The debate is often very defensive and divisive. This is inevitable as it's about food – such a very fundamental thing, characterised by desire, habit, culture, identity and passion. It also often involves strong moral stances, which can cause feelings of guilt and defensiveness.

---

45 see for example 'The Vegetarian Myth' by Lierre Keith, or Peter Gelderloos' pamphlet 'Veganism, why not?'.
46 It's very worth engaging with the ideas put forward by intersectional veganism – there are some great blogs e.g. www.intersectionalvegan.com.

Beyond probably easily agreeing that industrial animal farming is awful, there is a basic ideological clash over the value of animal life and whether it's 'natural and normal' for humans to use and kill animals for food. The fact that debating 'what's natural' is never the easiest or most conclusive starting point aside, this is a big ethical question that can and should be discussed, but can't be forced. It's also not necessarily black or white; humans have a relationship with animals, and you can draw the boundary between symbiotic beneficial relationships and exploitation in different ways.

More practical concerns are around sustainability or nutrition. From a nutritionist's perspective, it's fairly obvious that a Western diet full of processed foods, a large amount of vegetable oils and little diversity is detrimental to health, whether meat-centred or meat-free. Beyond that and with current knowledge, no one diet is best – different ways of eating will suit different people depending on their genetics, lifestyles, enzymes, metabolism, and state of their digestive systems. With a few individual exceptions, it's entirely possible to eat very well and cover all needs with a vegan or an omnivorous diet, with a few things that you would want to watch out for (e.g. avoiding processed meats, eating enough fruit and veg, getting Vitamin B12).

Simon Fairlie's collection of essays, *'Meat – a benign extravagance'* published in 2010 is an interesting assessment of vegan diets within a more sustainable food system. He makes some good points, including the efficiencies that some animal use allows for (e.g. using manure[47], grazing on land not suited for arable use, or the increased need for land to grow green manures for fertilising without animal agricualture), but his arguments aren't really conclusive. His calculations for theoretical land requirements of different food systems shows vegan permaculture to be quite advantageous, with fairly intense use of arable land, but 8.4 million 'spare' hectares, compared to only 2.4 million in livestock permaculture. The disadvantage, according to Fairlie, is that in the vegan permaculture scenario, we are left with unused grassland. I can't see why this is a bad thing! Especially considering the impact grazing has had on our hillsides, destabilising soils and causing flooding[48].

---

47 Phosphorus is one of the essential soil building nutrients and phosphorus fertilisers are based on a finite resource in danger of depletion. Fairlie argues we should be building more closed systems that use livestock waste for phosphorus, but this is not the only option – see the Vegan Organic Network, or Gerwin (2009), *Phosophorus Matters II* (http://permaculturenews.org/ 2009/07/23/phosphorus-matters-ii-keeping-phosphorus-on-farms/) for ideas that don't depend on animal agriculture, e.g. mycorrhizal funghi, biochar, and using bird and bat droppings.

48 See George Monbiot (2013) http://www.monbiot.com/ 2013/05/30/ sheepwrecked/).

We're probably all a little bit hung up on a romantic idea of sheep roaming our hillsides and mixed farming – the (non-capitalist) small farm with a couple of cows and chickens running around based on our Fisher Price farmyard set and a lost dream of a simpler, more self sufficient life. Some are lucky enough to be able to make this dream a reality with a bit of land and time to work it. Some dream bigger and try to develop new, sustainable ways of mixed agriculture. From the same sentiment, some might see veganism as a frankly alienated and disconnected response. However, we are also in constant evolution, and need to respond to a world on the brink of collapse. With even the UN concluding that a global shift to a vegan diet is vital to respond to world hunger, fossil fuel dependency, environmental destruction and the impact of climate change[49], we need to find new ways of maintaining a connection to the land and our traditions while moving away from animal agriculture and managing our natural resources responsibly. This also means not just replacing butter with factory processed palm oil based margarine, or venison with expensive imported ingredients, but treading exciting new paths.

To get back to individual consumption, our ideologically entrenched debating is just not helping. It's a familiar journey: discovering veganism in response to animal cruelty, to soon realise that this is a limited response to a food system that is wrong on so many levels. Living in industrial capitalism means contributing to exploitation,

49 UNEP (2010) *Assessing the environmental impacts of consumption and production*. Report.

death and destruction on a daily basis, and our life is constant compromise. We work to earn money and buy things in shops and pay rent and taxes, and we contribute to and uphold our exploitative, destructive capitalist system on a daily basis. If we choose to care, we have to constantly navigate difficult choices. 'Purity' is neither desirable nor possible (as Gelderloos puts it).

This is quite overwhelming, and can cause and reinforce defensive responses: in the one camp, focusing on veganism as a solution, in the other, rejecting consumer choice altogether and making jokes about bacon, with an equally defensive ideology. Our current discourse doesn't allow for much else[50].

I've had so many discussions with friends about exactly this struggle. Food is emotive, and we are very easily confused and conflicted over food choice. A vegan with strong enough motivation may not feel this conflict, and will happily choose plant foods. But those who aren't fully morally opposed to animal use, or for example aren't sure whether soy milk made with imported beans is any better than locally farmed cows milk[51], are likely to just not be motivated enough to refuse industrially farmed animal products on a daily basis, even if they disagree with the methods and consequences.

---

50 Disregarding the liberal campaigning approach of 'eat more vegan foods yay whoop', as that doesn't go much beyond reinforcing vegan consumerism.
51 This is just an example – it's really not the only choice you have.

I'm talking on an individual level. This doesn't mean closing down the discussion. It's important to be encouraging veganism, promoting sustainable plant foods, and challenging industrial animal farming. However, there's much harm done in making people feel guilty and like they have to make certain, correct choices, or giving yourself a hard time.

Personally, I'm not sure whether using animals for food is ethical or not, but I *feel* like I don't want to. I have an emotional response - I know I can't kill an animal for food myself, and hearing dairy cows crying for their calves that have been taken away is upsetting. Lacking the full conviction, I sometimes 'lapse' on dairy or eggs. Nevertheless, I prefer to promote and eat and engage with vegan food. And if asked, I'll say I prefer eating vegan, to help promote the idea and increase my opportunities of enjoying plant based foods. Is that a cop out? Yes - I was a consistent vegan for about 20 years, then found myself in the countryside, removed from a vegan community and my motivation waning. Rather than throw the baby out with the bathwater, as I've seen many ex-vegans do, I've made some compromises. Sometimes I need to rein it in as the exceptions slowly become the norm, and I need to remind myself that I want to make better food choices, but I continually try. And I can always do with encouragement, but I really don't want to be judged on this.

One of the reasons I know I've struggled with being vegan was having strict rules around food. **Restraint eating** was originally coined by Herman and Mack[52] and describes imposing rules on your eating and constantly fighting temptation, leading you to not be able to 'hear' your own internal hunger and satiety signals, and easily losing control when allowed to. A typical example of the effect of restraint eating is the *'I'm on a diet but I just had a bit of cake and broke my rule, I might as well have all the cake and some booze and chocolate too now'*. Some people may have very strong empathy with animals and don't require cognitive restraint to eat consistently vegan. But for those who aren't as strongly motivated or who feel muddled, a lot of cognitive restraint may be at work, with a 'lapse' meaning failure, and that their whole diet's been pointless.

"Overwhelmed by choice, by the dim threat of mortality that lurks beneath any wrong choice, people crave rules from outside themselves, and successful heroes to guide them to safety. (...) To eat without restriction, on the other hand, is to risk being unclean, and to beat your own uncertain path. It is admitting your mortality, your limitations and messiness as a biological creature, while accepting the freedoms and pleasures of eating, and taking responsibility for choosing them." (Michelle Allison (2017) *Eating Towards Immortality*[53])

---

52 Herman and Mack (1975) *Restrained and Unrestrained Eating*, Journal of Personality 43 (4).
53 https://www.theatlantic.com/health/archive/2017/02/eatin g-toward-immortality/515658/

Unrestrained eating doesn't mean eating mindlessly, but making our own choices, that are compassionate, aware, relevant and work for us as individuals. Developments such as a bigger role for intersectional critiques[54], body positive veganism, climate change related food activism, the growth of inventive plant based cookery, and more diversity in veganism as it becomes more 'mainstream', all give us hope that we are on a path to build a more positive anti-capitalist food culture and movement. This movement can *include* veganism and the communities that have grown around veganism, rather than veganism being a separate and polarising single issue, a pretentious lifestyle thing, mere consumerism offering more added value for food corporations, or another diet that you can succeed or fail at.

Food choice stories

"I've been a vegetarian for about 30 years and have no intention of changing. My eating during the day can be quite patchy. It takes quite a bit of effort to stop my work and make something proper for lunch. My work involves high concentration and when I'm in a flow state it can be hard to break it to eat or drink. The evening is when I'll eat a good meal. I take turns to cook with two other* people on various days, we eat together, talk and share the washing up. Food always has fresh veg, a protein, some starch, sometimes a pudding. Flavour, food that looks good, is of good quality, things that we all really enjoy eating, these are important things.

---

54 e.g. at the 2016 London Vegan Fair

I don't use much in the way of processed food. I eat plenty of food in the week that is vegan, but I wouldn't want this to be my diet all the time. There are many dishes with lacto-ovo ingredients that I like very much and which taste good to me, make me feel good in my body, and have pleasant associations (hot chocolate and buttery toast in the winter, my girlfriend's macaroni cheese, for example). I would like to see the end of animal cruelty and its industrialisation and I struggle with the ethics of eating animal products.

I think of veganism as a restrictive diet. I grew up with my body under surveillance in a culture that was always hectoring me to lose weight and restrict how I eat. One of the reasons I originally became a vegetarian was a hope that it would help me become thin. It didn't! Because of my history, I think becoming a vegan would give me an eating disorder. I'm uncomfortable with the moral content of veganism. I really dislike the healthism and self-righteousness that I see in some vegans; as a survivor of diet culture I want to try and avoid placing a heavy moral burden on the things I eat.

I live in a place where it's easy to eat really good, cheap, south Indian vegetarian and vegan food. I enjoy mooching around the gentrified vegan supermarkets that I find in other parts of London, but I rarely buy anything. I get overwhelmed by the variety, the highly processed nature of it turns me off, as does the drabness, and it's usually very pricy. Still, it seems that lentil chips are now a thing! I associate veganism with hipsters, rich people, kinds of citizenship and social cleansing that I don't want to be a part of. When I think about it like this I see veganism as a first world affectation. I think my ambivalence is about how it is developing in the West, how some people approach it as an identity, I'll be interested to see how that develops and hope a more critical understanding might emerge in time."

Charlotte Cooper, psychotherapist and cultural worker, charlottecooper.net

"Like many people I approached veganism from vegetarianism and this in turn came from spending a lot of time in DIY and Punk subcultures which discuss and promote animal rights, with the usual thoughts and perspectives on empathy and causing harm, responsibility as well as wider ecological and environmental concerns, but also the joy and creativity that came from having to be inventive with food.

Over the years my relationship to certain aspects of veganism has become more complicated and critical. The most contentious aspect of it is the moralised superiority that comes from certain vegans which alternates from a smug condescension to a vitriolic absolutism that verges, for me at least, on intolerant fundamentalism. Quite simply, I don't think veganism is a lifestyle choice that can be extended to all people on the planet, particularly not with an overarching moral viewpoint. For me a vegan outlook that doesn't at least try to come to terms with a complicated and layered structural approach to understanding animal agriculture (and the economic reasons as to why it is produced this way and why animals are reduced to bio-fodder) is extremely limited.

The recent development of the 'veganism as health' movement from a more bourgeois and middle-class perspective also has its problems – although it's certainly great to have more vegan options I feel it's also another part of the problematic 'Slimness is Health/Good Health is a Virtue' marketing drive that feels like it's everywhere at the moment, and it goes without saying is extremely privileged.

These criticisms in place – veganism is still important to me, and I've reflected long and hard on this. Recently I had a year of 'flexible veganism' where basically if I was somewhere I couldn't get a vegan option, I'd have the vegetarian one and thoroughly enjoyed it. My prime motivation was that I felt that I was 'missing out' on something, that as a restriction on my diet it was becoming a bit of a barrier to new experiences in life and that my individual actions had absolutely zero affect on the gigantic economic machine that rears animals for food production, so what was the point? The point, I realised, was that sometimes it's important to have perspectives and commitments that aren't just based on pragmatism, or economic arguments. Sometimes you need to focus on things or a way of being that feels like it's a representation of a principal or an ideal. To have a way of existing in and negotiating the world that you offer out as a beacon to illuminate new ways of thinking, reflecting and relating to the world. I will always negotiate and renegotiate my perspectives on veganism but I know that it remains an important, internal drive and thus, still feels worthwhile to engage in over a decade after I first made my choice to stop eating animals."

Michael Douglas

"I don't have a very good memory, as anyone who knows me will tell you, but I can vividly recall lying on my bed in my damp post-graduate basement flat more than 10 years ago, tearing through Vegan Freak by Bob and Jenna Torres. I read this book in one sitting and felt like I had come home. A strange, almost ecclesiastical phrase* I know, but I really could have been shouting hallelujah, it all made a lot of sense. I had been vegetarian on and off since I was 11 years old, when the visceral experience of meat eating had just been too much for me, though I'm sure I couldn't have told you why.

I think it was actually the experience over my university years of letting my partner throw some prawns in our stir-fry, or eating a few Haribo sweets here and there, and just kind of shrugging and chowing down that got me thinking. Why was I vegetarian? Perhaps I shouldn't bother with this label if it didn't really mean anything to me or those around me, let alone any being further outside my human experience.

Back to the same dingy basement flat and there I am, eating my cornflakes and soya milk, ready to cry, thinking, 'shit, I have to eat this for the rest of my life' and 'oh man, what have I done?' Yes, I had decided to go vegan overnight, because it's my way, it's my personality. My friends couldn't believe their good luck as I chucked out all my leather shoes and woollen jumpers. I couldn't believe my bad luck at how much soya milk sucked.

Behind all of this a fire had been lit inside me. It felt to me that going vegan would be the only way to compassionately react to what I had read about how animals were treated in the dairy and egg industries, something I previously knew next to nothing about. Vegan Freak was illuminating, not just in terms of large scale animal abuse, but of systemic oppression that I had never even considered. Such is the privilege of the human animal. It's this light that keeps me vegan, I can't turn it off, and I wouldn't want to. I sometimes wish I could shine it more brightly, but I think that everyone who makes their tiny choices and shares it is doing something meaningful to extend compassion to human and non-human animals alike. The growing, shifting community, of which we were a tiny super-connected part in that moment in time, is what keeps me motivated for eternity."
* I can only apologise for the preponderance of this sort of idiom in my writing: I was raised in the church, but that's a whole other story.

Hannah Webb, donutsandbolts.com

Basic sponge cake:

400g self raising flour
200g caster sugar
200ml vegetable oil
300ml soy milk, or 200ml soy milk and 100ml water
1 tsp bicarbonate of soda
1 tsp lemon juice or white wine vinegar

From our cookbook *Another Dinner is Possible*. Enough to fill 2-3 loaf tins, 1 large deep baking tray, or use 2/3 of the recipe for a 20cm round tin
Preheat oven to 180-200°C/Gas Mark 5-6. Grease the tins. Sift the flour (for **chocolate cake:** 50g cocoa + 350g flour) into a mixing bowl and add caster sugar. Mix together and stir in the oil.
Mix the soy milk, bicarbonate of soda and lemon juice or vinegar separately, then add to the mix, stir until smooth. Bake for about 30 minutes or until a knife stuck in comes out clean.
Vary it by simply adding ingredients such as spices, grated carrot, mashed banana, nuts, dates, orange juice and zest, etc...

Raw brownie:

1 cup of cashews
1 cup walnuts
½ cup cocoa
24 dates
a pinch of salt
¼ cup cacao nibs
a dash of maple syrup

Whizz in a food processor, and press down into a greased tin, then set in the fridge.

Almond and date balls: Whizz (in a food processor) equal amounts of dates and almonds or other nuts with a bit of peanut or other nut butter, ½ tbsp maca if handy, cinnamon, vanilla, and a pinch of salt. Press into balls.

Coconut whipped cream: You'll find recipes for this everywhere online now but this is how I make it. Chill a tin of coconut milk (full fat) overnight. Before taking it out, chill a plastic mixing bowl. Then carefully open the tin, and remove just the thick creamy bit (it should have separated). You can keep the watery bit for smoothies or cooking. Beat for a bit with a mixer, then add about half a cup sifted icing sugar (more if you like it sweet) and a splash of vanilla extract while continuing to beat.

Coconut macaroons (makes about 15):

¾ cup desiccated coconut
½ cup ground almonds
salt
vanilla or almond extract
1-2 tbsp syrup
2 tbsp coconut oil
40g dark chocolate (optional

In a food processor, mix the coconut, ground almonds, a pinch of salt, a dash of vanilla or almond extract, 1-2 tbsp syrup (maple, agave or golden), and melted coconut oil. The mixture should stick together when pressed (if not, add a tiny bit more syrup or oil). Form into small balls, and refrigerate for at least an hour.
I also like to dip them in melted chocolate and leave to set on baking paper in the fridge.

Truffles:

1 tin coconut milk
1 small chilli
1 cinnamon stick
salt
200g dark chocolate
2 tbsp coconut oil

Heat the coconut milk with the chilli, cinnamon and a pinch of salt. When hot, take off the heat and leave to steep for 20 mins. Remove the chili and cinnamon, then bring back to the near-boil, and then break in the dark chocolate and coconut oil. Whisk well, then pour to set it in a form (I use a small lined baking tray) and chill. Cut into pieces, then dust in cocoa.

Peanut frozen punch thing:

1 tin coconut milk
500ml soy milk
1 jar peanut butter
vanilla
nutmeg
1 tbsp cinnamon
3 tbsp molasses

Mike's sister Helen made this for us and it was delicious. For a whole lot, whizz the coconut milk, soy milk, peanut butter, a splash of vanilla, a bit of nutmeg, a large tbsp of cinnamon and molasses. Pour into a tupperware and freeze for at least 1 hour.

Avocado pudding (for 2):

1 large avocado
1 tbsp cocoa
3 tbsp coconut milk
bit of coconut oil
vanilla
2-3 tbsp maple or other syrup

Whizz everything in a food processor til smooth. Pour into individual glass pots and set in the refrigerator.

Raw berry cheesecake:

1 cup walnuts
¾ cup dates
2 cups cashew nuts
1 lemon
4-5 tbsp maple syrup
4 tbsp melted coconut oil
2 cups berries

Make the base from walnuts or other nuts (mixed, pecans, hazelnuts all work) whizzed up with dates and about 2 tbsp water. Spread into an 8" tin (ideally with removable base), pressing down evenly.

Soak cashew nuts in hot water for a few hours. Drain, then whizz in a food processor with the juice of one lemon, maple or other syrup, and melted coconut oil. Scoop about ½ – 2/3 of this on the base, smooth over and leave to set in a freezer for an hour or so. Whizz the rest with 2 cups of berries (I use about 200g frozen berry mix) and a pinch of cinnamon and vanilla extract. Pour onto the hardened base, and freeze again for another hour. Defrost for half an hour before serving.

For a cheaper version, and if you're not too fussed about it being raw or sugar free, you can also make the base with 200g digestive biscuits and 4 tbsp melted margarine, and replace 2/3 – 3/4 of the cashew nuts with a small banana and ½ pack (175g) silken tofu.

Pod Cafe's Coconut baileys

400ml coconut milk
200ml whiskey
50 ml syrup
2 tsp vanilla
1½ tsp cocoa
1½ tsp instant coffee

Dissolve the cocoa powder and instant coffee fully in 2 tbsp boiling water. Combine all the ingredients and gently blitz with a hand blender to combine, adding up to 150ml water as you go. Serve over ice. Will keep in a sealed container in the fridge for five days.

Our Food Cultures

Food choice in a capitalist food system is a complicated, political, social, and revolutionary issue affected by circumstance, access, class, and culture. We've got our stereotypes of the lower class, junk food, fried egg and beer subsisting burden to the NHS, overweight and on route to diabetes and an early death, vs the middle class health conscious family who enjoy their organic veg box and artisan foods and well designed cookbooks. We assume good food is reserved for those with money. What can we do to break down these stereotypes, go beyond well meaning food activism that doesn't address most people's realities, and make good food accessible to all?

As with many things, surely the answer lies in a collective, revolutionary, open minded approach with a rejection of capitalism, and an awareness of privilege and the many barriers to good health and nutrition.

Teaching people to cook is not much use if they have shit kitchens or equipment. Preaching veganism and that eating animals is terrible is not much use if you feel completely alienated by vegan culture or you don't feel empowered to make that kind of choice. Extolling the virtues and better taste of food from farmers markets is not much use if people are used to budgeting around incredibly cheap, shit food. Being scathing about junkfood and going on about local, seasonal and fancy restaurants is not much use to anyone strapped for cash and just serves to reinforce divisions. Being discerning about which products you buy just allows for further capitalist expansion. Also, taking photos of your dinner may be a celebration of food and should be a nice thing, but not really very cool if it's more about showing off than actual enjoyment and appreciation. Unfortunately the more visible expressions of any kind of alternative food culture in the West seem largely individualistic, well-intentioned but not very revolutionary or easily co-opted, and/or extremely privileged. But there is also much scope to find genuine, humble and more accessible food projects and growing and cooking passion.

If you look beyond the Borough Market Artisan Cheese, there are amazing and inspiring grassroots food activists aplenty – people making allotment gardening accessible and more interesting, food co-ops that actually improve access to food for people who have had to rely on cornershops, growers and food producers coming up with exciting new sustainable methods from vegan permaculture to urban agroecology and producing good food without gimmicks or capitalist noise, people helping others learn to cook and improve diets without patronising, people talking about and working on health and well-being in a political context.

The Real Junk Food Project set up 'pay as you feel' cafes, cooking with reclaimed surplus food from the food chain. therealjunkfoodproject.org

Incredible Edible Originally set up in Todmorden and now expanded to many other cities, this urban gardening project has been hugely successful and inspiring. www.incredible-edible-todmorden.co.uk

Growing Support is a social enterprise offering social and therapeutic activities for older people, with gardening clubs and more. http://growingsupport.co.uk/

Brighton Moulsecoombe Forest Garden has grown from a community allotment to working with schools, offering training, and campaigning to save local woodlands. http://seedybusiness.org/

Kitchen on Prescription offer cookery support, with the resources that you have, through GP referrals. http://www.wellspringhlc.org.uk/kitchen-on-prescription/

La Via Campensina is a global peasant movement for food sovereignty, campaigning for sustainable production and against corporate control of the food system. https://viacampesina.org/en/

"Food sovereignty is the right of peoples to healthy and culturally appropriate food produced through ecologically sound and sustainable methods, and their right to define their own food and agriculture systems."
- Declaration of Nyeleni (2007)

This can also begin at home. One of my favourite pastimes is cooking for large groups of people, not in some kind of dinner party setting, but bringing people together over a shared meal of delicious and hopefully inventive and exciting food made from simple plant based ingredients. Social eating is a rarity and offers a glimpse of enjoying food beyond the microwaved meal eaten alone, the stress of making food for all the family, the expensive meal at the restaurant where you don't make eye contact with other guests, the hastily eaten sandwich at your desk at work.

And the simple act of breaking down the disconnect where your food comes from is a vital step – get your hands in some soil, grow something, help out at a farm or allotment and experience first hand what it means to obtain food. Out of the supermarket, into the fields to overcome the alienation of the capitalist world, and to know what we are fighting for.

But what about your own individual food choices? They matter – your food culture matters (more than your consumption). It's worth taking time, care and putting thought into what food you use, grow, cook and eat. There is not one right way, but the right way for you, which should reflect your values, and which you should be able to enjoy.

These values can be contradictory and might need to be balanced, e.g. a value of living simply and with little money vs. a rejection of cheap imported food; or a value of rejecting animal cruelty vs a value of multicultural diversity and cuisines[55]. And choices are made in the context of material circumstances – access to food, budget, mental health, lifestyle, feelings of entitlement. Navigating and surviving industrial capitalism is difficult for most of us, and it's not easy to be consistent, and as discussed in the previous chapter, will always involve compromise. It's not cool to just shirk your responsibility about food choice, not give a damn and be lazy, and it's important to encourage each other to try our best, but we are more than just consumers, and there are more valuable things we could be doing than spending all our time judging ourselves or each other.

Values can also be related to cultural values and your sense of place. For some, this means hankering for old fashioned small scale mixed farming with a few cows and pigs, or embracing traditional pastimes such as hunting,

---

55 e.g. I have some 'cultural vegan exceptions' when traveling to new places (though I can't bring myself to eat meat). I dislike the slightly imperialist feeling of imposing my own values onto someone else's culture and insisting on vegan food when there are few options, as well feeling I'm denying myself new experiences I'm curious about. But, I also think it's good for vegans to travel and try to be vegan in other countries. Personally, my motivation to be open to other cultures means compromising on how I feel about eating animal products in this case.

cheese-making, or cooking in loads of butter instead of dodgy vegetable oils. And this may well be from a genuine passion, and not thoughtless and offhand cruelty, even though it's difficult to relate to when you strongly empathise with animals yourself.

One more approach I'd like to mention here that I think has a lot of promise in helping to navigate nutrition information, conflicting values, and the guilt and shame rather than joy we might feel about eating is **intuitive eating**. It was developed as a variation of mindful eating (which you've probably heard of), mainly in response to breaking down diet mentalities and actually developing healthy habits more naturally. It's based on rediscovering your own intrinsic motivation for and your body's internal physical cues to eating and living healthily, with self compassion. We are born intuitive eaters! However, along the way many of us learn it's not ok to trust our emotions or to trust our bodies when it comes to food. We may grow up being told it's a sin to waste food and so have to continue eating even when we're full. Or there may be practical issues that impinge on our relationship with food, such as not having enough to eat so we eat as much as we can when there is food available, whether or not we're full.

 That makes a lot of sense as a survival strategy, but gets confusing in a supermarket aisle. Restraint eating, strict dietary regimes, or forbidding certain foods may work for some very few people, but

for most, it means overriding and silencing our bodies' biological hunger and satiety signals, and giving in to 'temptation' and then feeling guilty repeatedly. The main principles of intuitive eating are:

Reject the diet mentality – also the lingering 'hope' that the perfect diet will sort you out. Get angry at the lies you've been told, and learn to trust in yourself and your own choices. This can be very difficult and usually requires a whole paradigm shift – but is a vital step to developing intuitive eating.

Honour your hunger – Pay attention to your biological hunger signals and don't ignore them, avoid excessive hunger, and eat when you need to. Hunger is a primal and powerful thing. The experience affects your whole body, preoccupies your mind, and even affects your genes – e.g. people with a genetic history of famine are prone to preferentially storing food as fat and burning less energy.

Make peace with food – Give yourself permission to eat, unconditionally. When things are forbidden they can trigger intense cravings. This doesn't mean EAT EVERYTHING IN SIGHT, it means: figure out what you really want or don't want, and why – don't just make blind rules for yourself that you will find hard to stick to, or just see foods as good or bad.

Challenge the food police – within yourself, that makes you feel guilty about bad foods. Observant and nurturing self talk vs rules or rebellion.

Feel your fullness – Listen for body signals that tell you you're no longer hungry. Learn to recognise when you are comfortably full, or when you're no longer enjoying what you're eating.

Discover the satisfaction factor – Reject the puritan notion that getting pleasure from food is some kind of sin. Enjoy eating. Broaden your palate. Ask yourself what you really want to eat right now. Eat varied. Eat in a nice environment, sit at a table, take time. Savour foods.

Cope with your emotions without using food – find ways to comfort yourself or reward yourself without using food. Food can comfort and distract, but it doesn't solve problems. Learn to recognise emotional eating patterns and work to find alternatives.

Respect your body – Love your body, and this will help you take care of it, and learn to listen to it. If you struggle with this – as most people in our thin-ideal and body-judgmental world do – engage in positive self talk and do nice things for your body.

Exercise – for the fun of it, and not just as the duty to hit the gym and burn calories! Exercise includes daily active living (walking, gardening, taking the stairs, kicking a ball around) and should be enjoyable, not a chore.

Honour your health with gentle nutrition – this doesn't mean the perfect diet or nutrition by numbers, but making food choices that honour your health and taste buds.

Some people are lucky enough to be naturally intuitive eaters, but for many of us it's a difficult – and possibly unimaginable – journey. To me, the idea that your body knows best – learning to trust it and helping yourself make positive decisions around eating rather than feeling the need to stick to strict rules or a diet plan, feels like an extension of the kind of autonomous choices I enjoy being able to make in other parts of life.

While the hope of global social revolution remains just a glimmer, especially in the face of a highly resilient capitalist system coping with multiple crises while further cementing inequalities and shifting towards the right or even outright fascism, our day to day revolutions involve more practical and immediate action. Solidarity. Improving our access to resources. Resisting corporate and state encroachment and repression. Defending wilderness and defending our communities. Learning and sharing skills and experiences. Trying to keep true to our ideals in the ways we live and organise. Coming back again to the initial thought that what we eat is so significant to society, analysing, organising around, and applying changes to what we eat and how is hugely relevant. Thinking about our food is much bigger than just individual preference and consumerism - it's thinking about how we organise society and humanity's major activities and impact. And taking care of ourselves and the world shouldn't be marked by guilt, denial and judgment, but be pleasurable and constructive.

Building a more efficient, sustainable and healthy food system to feed the world could involve:

new methods (urban farming[56], agroecology[57], aquaponics), developing new crops, using land efficiently, and building diversity, supporting research into sustainable agriculture rather than high input industrialised or GM crops

➤ more efficient, small scale farming, food production and use of land[58], including crop rotations and using natural cycles and crop rotation to build soil

➤ less use of artificial fertilisers, pesticides and herbicides and more natural soil building and pest control

➤ switching from a dependency on fossil fuels to renewables and more efficient use of energy

➤ more localised production and distribution, less importing

➤ less convenience and out of season foods, but fresher and tastier produce (in the UK, probably more root vegetables and cabbage and less mangos)

➤ less processed and packaged food

---

56 See accounts of post-fossil-fuel transition in the Cuban food system for inspiration
57 Agricultural systems that take ecological and social factors into account
58 See Badgley et al (2007) *Organic Agriculture and global food supply*. Renewable Agriculture and Food Systems 22 for a discussion of how small scale farming can produce as high or higher yields as industrial farming.

> more people involved in growing food (and maybe less people sending emails in offices)

> moving from billions of grain fed animals to a just few pasture fed

> cutting down on middlemen and breaking down corporate control of seeds, food production, and distribution

> less waste – we could have up to 40% more food to eat!

> overthrowing government and total social revolution

Thankfully, as Colin Tudge is known to say, good cooking goes hand in hand with more benign and sustainable agriculture and good practises such as smaller scale farming, localised systems and more diversity. As we try to be the people we want to be – practising mutual aid, addressing privilege and offering solidarity, trying to be fair and kind, and resisting and revolting – the efforts we make to also improve our food culture can help inform and build a better food system for the future.

Further Reading:
Tribole and Resch (2012) Intuitive Eating
Holt-Gimenez and Patel (2009) Food Rebellions! Crisis and the Hunger for Justice

How to cook a soup:

2 onions * 1 stick celery * 1 small carrot * 500g floury potatoes * 500g vegetables * 1 litre stock

Soups are a great and easy way to get your head around flavour combinations, use up veg and whip up a quick dinner in little time. And homecooked soup's much better than tinned/shop bought that will have a lot of salt to intensify the taste that's lost in keeping it. Soups work especially well with two ingredients that complement each other.

This is our basic vegetable soup recipe (for 6), that's mostly thickened by potato but can also be based on any other root vegetable. Then see suggested flavour combos below, or try your own!

Chop and cook 2 onions, a stick of celery and a small carrot if you have in a bit of oil, until softening. Add any spices at this point, e.g. cumin, thyme, ground coriander etc, and a couple of chopped cloves of garlic if you like. Now add your veg – the basic recipe would be up to 500g floury potatoes and 500g vegetables; this might be less if it's very light/watery veg (use at least a fist-sized amount of veg per person as a rough guide) and a different ratio of potatoes/veg. You can also roast your veg first if it's suited to roasting, this adds a lot of flavour!

Cover with up to 1 litre veg stock (you can use boullion, stock cubes, or make your own with scraps!) to just about cover the veg. Bring to the boil and then simmer until the veg is breaking down. If you are using veg that has a shorter cooking time (greens for example) wait, and add them a bit before the end. Season to taste (depending on how salty the stock is it might not need much salt) and blend if you like. You can add a bit of soy cream, coconut milk or extra stock at this point if it's too thick – you can always thin a soup down but not easily thicken it so don't overdo adding liquid at the start!

Finally, serve garnished with a bit of soy or cashew cream, fresh herbs, toasted seeds, chopped spring onion, or a dusting of spices to make it all more appealing!

Good combos:

With potato base: Potato and herbs, potato and watercress (and/or spinach), leek and potato, roasted garlic and apple, potato and green cabbage, potato and kale, roasted hazelnut, celeriac and apple ...

With just a few spuds: celery and cashew, courgette and tarragon, pea and mint, broad bean and mint, fennel and lemon (use fennel seeds too), jerusalem artichoke and cashews, broccoli, carrot and dill, asparagus, sweet potato and orange, sweet potato and spinach, curry spiced parsnip, parsnip and apple...

With other veg: roasted butternut squash, carrot and coriander, cauliflower and almond, carrot and apple, pumpkin with nutmeg and cinnamon, carrot and orange (use orange zest and the juice)...

Salad Lunch Joy: I often throw together a quick salad for lunch. The possibilities are endless, it just takes a few staple ingredients at hand and any veg you got in the fridge, and you'll quickly find combinations that work well for you (and which are gross and don't work at all...).

Choose a base of either a cooked grain (e.g. leftover rice, or pasta) or lentils, shredded cabbage for more of a slaw, or greens.

Then add veg at hand – salad veg like radishes or sweetcorn, chopped avocados, chopped spring onion, grated carrot, courgette or beetroot, fennel, blanched broccoli or kale, leftover roast veg, strips of pepper, cucumber chunks.

Then a bit of crunch – toasted seeds, nuts, or croutons.

And if it would suit, extras for satiety and protein, such as drained and well rinsed tinned beans, a few chunks of fried tofu, some cooked or roasted potato, white or sweet. Grain salads especially can also benefit from extras like olives, sundried tomatoes, a bit of seasweed, or capers.

And finally a delicious dressing for flavouring! Done!

Delicious dressings – I'm not going to bore you with how to make a basic vinaigrette (1:4 vinegar to oil), but here are some others I like.

Miso dressing: Whizz up 1 tbsp rice vinegar with 1 tsp dijon mustard, 1 tbsp (ideally light) miso, and a dash of water. Add 1 tsp tamari or soy sauce, 1 tbsp toasted sesame oil and 3 tbsp veg oil and whizz to emulsify. Optional extras: a clove of garlic or a bit of ginger, a bit of fresh coriander.

You can also try subbing the miso with tahini; add a bit of sugar or syrup in that case.

Tahini dressing: Blend equal amounts tahini and water (about 3 tbsp each) with the juice of 1 large lemon, 2 cloves of garlic, salt and pepper, and a drizzle of maple syrup if you have it. A bit of tamari is also nice, and/or extra sesame seeds or a pinch of ground cumin.

Engevita dressing: Blend 1 tbsp cider vinegar with 1 tsp tamari, 1 tsp dijon mustard, 1 heaped tbsp engevita, a bit of pepper and 4 tbsp veg or light olive oil.

Vegan Mayo: Blend 125ml soy milk or a mix of soy milk and soy cream with a little squeeze of lemon juice and 1 tsp mustard (either wholegrain or dijon) in a food processor, blender, or with a hand blender. Start adding 150-250ml light olive oil or a neutral vegetable oil (or a mix) in a slow stream while continuing to blend. Season to taste, and add stuff like garlic or fresh chopped herbs at the end if you like.

Joey's Ginger Dressing: Grate and inch or two of peeled fresh ginger, then whizz with 2 tsp tomato puree, juice of 2 limes, 2 tsp tamari, 1 tsp sugar, 2 cloves of garlic, and fresh coriander to taste.

Walnut dressing: Blend 3 cloves of garlic with a handful of walnuts, 1 tbsp cider vinegar, salt, 1 tsp mustard, 1 tsp maple syrup or similar, adding olive oil bit by bit until creamy.

Pod cafe dressing: Blend 1 tsp (vegan) Thai green curry paste, 1 1/2 tbsp olive oil, 1/2 tbsp pumpkin seed oil, juice of half a lime, 1/2 tbsp sweet chilli sauce, and a generous tbsp of tahini.

Sushi coleslaw: For a twist on coleslaw, finely shred cabbage (white, red, pointy, Chinese) lightly salt and then massage with your hands a bit, just to soften then. Add grated carrot/and or courgette, finely shredded spring onion, fresh coriander if you have, some sesame seeds, and a little bit of shredded sushi ginger. Mix with a miso salad dressing and garnish with roasted peanuts.

Massaged kale: Strip washed kale leaves off their hard stalks into a large bowl. Add a splash of lemon juice and salt, and tear and massage with your fingers until it softens. Add a splash of olive oil.

Massaged kale salad (for about 6): Break up a head of cauliflower into florets, toss in a bit of oil and roast in a hottish oven until soft and browned (about 20 minutes). You can also roast a sweet potato, cut into chunks, to add in. Massage a large bunch of kale as above, adding lemon juice and salt, then dress with a bit of wholegrain mustard and olive oil. Toast a handful of flaked almonds or cashews, and toss them in with the kale along with the roasted veg.

Massaged kale peanut coleslaw: Mix massaged kale, finely sliced cabbage (which also benefits from being massaged a bit with some salt) and grated carrot, and a few toasted flaked almonds, roasted peanuts, or seeds. Make a dressing by blending 1 tbsp peanut butter, the juice of 1 lime, a dash of rice vinegar, 1 clove of garlic and a bit of chopped ginger, a dash of tamari and a bit of fruit syrup (agave or maple) and toasted sesame oil, and a tiny bit of sriacha sauce if you have.

Avocado Pesto (for 2): Blend 1 ripe avocado, a handful of basil, 1 clove of garlic, 1 tbsp lemon juice, and salt and pepper. Add 2-3 tbsp olive oil gradually while blending. Serve in pasta with some halved cherry tomatoes and shredded baby spinach or peas.

Hannah's Turmeric Tahini sauce

Delicious over roast veg – whisk 3 tbsp light tahini with the juice of a lemon, adding water bit by bit until you have the consistency you like. Finely grate a nobble of fresh turmeric and add, along with a tbsp of maple or other syrup, a small clove of garlic, minced, and a dash of tamari.

Leeks and greens (for 6):

2 leeks or onions
Veg or coconut oil
Large bag of greens and ½ small cabbage
2 cloves garlic, 1 inch ginger
1 tin coconut milk
1 tbsp tamari
½ lime or lemon

Cook the sliced leeks or onion in the oil for a few minutes. Add the shredded greens, cabbage and garlic and ginger, and stir fry for 5 minutes over medium high heat. Add the coconut milk, and bring to the boil. Simmer for a few then add the tamari and squeeze of lime or lemon juice to serve.

Tomato tamarind salad (for 6):

1 red or white onion
6 tomatoes
3-4 tbsp tamarind paste
2-3 tbsp sugar
1 lime
1 tsp each salt and chaat masala spice
400g tin chickpeas
fresh coriander
100g sev or similar

A take on the Indian streetfood Bhel Puri. Quarter, then thinly slice the onion, and chop the tomatoes into cubes (you can also de-seed them first).

Simmer the tamarind paste with a bit of water and sugar for a few minutes (then strain if it's the type that has bits). Add the juice of the lime, salt, and chaat masala spice if you have. Mix everything together just before serving, along with the drained and rinsed chickpeas, a good handful of fresh coriander, chopped, and the sev – crispy gram flour nibbles, or puffed rice, or some broken poppadum.

You can also add a bit of cubed cooked potato, or a bit of green or garlic chutney.

Cauliflower tabbouleh:

1 cauliflower
2 red onion
½ bunch each parsley and mint
a few chives or spring onion
1 cucumbers
1 lemon
olive oil

In a food processor, whizz up the cauliflower broken into florets, then finely chop and add the onion, herbs and de-seeded cucumber. Dress with the lemon juice, salt and pepper to taste and a generous drizzle of olive oil. Another one based on something from Jess' marvellous Pod Cafe.

Layered sweet potato and cauliflower bake (for 6):

Veg oil
1 cauliflower
1 large sweet potato or 2 small
1 onion
2 cloves garlic
1 bunch kale/greens
½ tin coconut milk
2 tbsp nutritional yeast
salt to taste (up to 1 tsp), pinch nutmeg, 1 tsp thyme and 1 tsp rosemary
Flaked almonds or breadcrumbs (optional)

Break the cauliflower up into florets, toss in a bit of oil and roast on a baking sheet in a medium hot oven until brown. Peel and slice the sweet potato, toss in oil, lay out on a deep casserole dish and roast as well, about 10 minutes.

Meanwhile, cook a chopped onion (or a small onion and a bit of sliced leek) in a bit of oil, then add garlic, then 1 bunch chopped washed kale or greens. When soft, add the rest of the ingredients, bring to the boil and cook down for 5 minutes.

Get the sweet potatoes out, lay the cauliflower over it, then the cooked greens. Sprinkle some flaked almonds or breadcrumbs over if you want, then bake for 15-20 minutes in a medium oven.

Miso broth (for 2):

5 cloves garlic
1 inch ginger
veg and sesame oil
1 small carrot
handful cabbage or broccoli
200g tofu or shii-

Perfect for when you have a cold or want a general anti-inflammatory and warming pick me up. Cook chopped garlic and ginger (plus optional chilli) in a mix of veg and sesame oil.

Add the carrot (cut into julienne slices, not rounds), and a handful of shredded

take mushrooms
turmeric, pepper
and sugar, and/or
a bit of seaweed
1 tbsp tamari or
soy sauce
1 tbsp white miso
rice vinegar
spring onion

cabbage or a few small florets of broccoli and cook for a couple mins. Then add the cubed tofu OR a handful of shii-take mushrooms, soaked in hot water for 20 minutes, drained and sliced. Plus a pinch of turmeric, pepper and sugar, and/or a bit of seaweed, e.g. wakame (all optional). Cover with 500-600ml water, plus tamari or soy sauce, and bring to the boil.

Simmer for 5 minutes or more if the mushrooms need it. Then stir in white miso, a dash of rice vinegar, and serve sprinkled with finely chopped spring onion.

Pod Cafe's Mighty Bean Burger (makes 8):

1 small fennel
1 small leek
2 cloves garlic
1/2 tbsp coconut
oil
1 cup cooked
quinoa
3 cups cooked
black beans
1/ tbsp cumin
1/2 tsp cayenne
pepper (more if
you like it hot)
1/2 tbsp Marigold

Preheat the oven to 180/ gas mark 8, and cook the diced fennel, leeks and garlic in the coconut oil until tender. Add the spices and fry until it just starts to stick then add a splash of water and take off the heat. Add to the beans and quinoa, adding in the bouillon, tamari and gram flour. Roughly blend with a stick blender to bind but leaving a few whole beans. Mix in the herbs and stir well. With wet hands roughly shape a handful of the burger mix and place on a greased

bouillon
1 tbsp tamari
2 tbsps gram flour
small handful of chopped chives and/or wild garlic
Sesame seeds to sprinkle

baking tray. Sprinkle the burgers with the sesame seeds and bake for 35-40 minutes until they are browned and crisp on the outside.

White bean gravy (for 6):

1 large onion
5 cloves of garlic
2 tbsp marge or veg oil
1 tsp fennel seed, thyme, rosemary, cumin, pepper
2 tins white beans
3 tbsp engevita
400ml stock
1 tbsp tamari
1 tbsp miso
1 tsp lemon juice

Gluten free, and the kind that you'd get in the US on biscuits, which are not cookies but savoury scone things. Also good with bangers and mash or on any root veg. Cook chopped onion and garlic in 2 tbsp marge or veg oil, until translucent. Add 1 tsp each fennel seed, thyme, rosemary, and cumin, plus a bit of pepper. Cook for a minute then add the drained white beans (butter, cannelini or even haricot – cannelini works best though), engevita, stock and tamari, and bring to the boil. Cook for about 5 minutes, then add miso and lemon juice, and blend.

Rice and peas (for 6):

1 small onion or 2 spring onions
1 clove garlic
2 cups rice
1 tin of kidney or other dark beans
1 tsp salt, a bit of pepper
1 tin coconut milk
1 tsp thyme

Use the liquid from the beans, the coconut milk and water to make up about 4 cups (1 litre) liquid. Fry the finely chopped onion and garlic in a bit of veg oil for a few minutes, then add the rice and give it a stir. Add the rest of the ingredients and bring to the boil. Get a lid on and simmer, with the occasional check/stir, until all the liquid's been absorbed – between 15 -30 minutes depending on the kind of rice you use.

Cashew cream: Soak 1 cup of unsalted cashews in 4 cups of boiling water for at least 6 hours. Drain, then blend in a blender or nutribullet adding cold water bit by bit as it runs, to the desired consistency, and a little bit of lemon juice or miso for flavour if you like.

Barley risotto (for 6):

Up to 2 litres stock
1 large onion
3 sticks celery
5 tbsp olive oil
2 cloves garlic
500g barley
1 glass white wine

Heat your stock – you can easily make your own with any veg scraps, making sure to include some onion, celery and carrot plus a bay leaf and salt. Keep it hot on a low heat while you cook the risotto. Fry the onion and celery in the oil until softish, add garlic, then the barley. Stir through, then add the wine and cook for a minute to evaporate

Salt and pepper
1 heaped tbsp margarine
4 tbsp soy or cashew cream

some of the alcohol. Keep the heat at medium, and start adding stock, bit by bit and always just enough to cover, letting it come to the boil after each addition and stirring often. Cook this way for about 30 minutes, then turn heat right down, cover, and let the risotto simmer for another 10 minutes. Season, add the margarine and cream. Extras: cook mushrooms or leeks with the onion at the start, add washed greens or peas near the end, or roasted squash.

Smoky paprika curry (for 4-6):

2 aubergines
Oil
1 large onion
2 cloves garlic
1 inch ginger
4 small tomatoes
Garam or tandoori masala, cumin, smoked paprika
Fresh coriander

Cut the aubergines into medium size cubes, and toss in salt and leave to drain for a bit. Rinse and dry then toss again in oil, then spread out on a baking sheet and roast in a hot oven until soft and brown (about 20 minutes).
Meanwhile, cook a chopped onion in some oil til soft. Add chopped garlic and ginger and cook a couple minutes, then 1 tsp each of the spices.
Add chopped tomatoes, and cook stirring often until soft. Stir in the roasted aubergine, and serve with chopped fresh coriander.

Farinata (for about 10):

500-600ml weak stock
200g gram flour
olive oil
roast veg
large handful fresh herbs
salt and pepper

A take on a chickpea flour pancake mutated into an egg-free Spanish tortilla, of sorts. Cheap, easy and tasty. Make a batter by whisking 500-600ml of weak stock, or water, into 200g gram/chickpea flour, add a glug of olive oil and leave to stand for at least 4 hours up to 12 (scrape off any foam that forms). Meanwhile, roast some veg (aubergines, peppers, potatoes, red onions, courgettes, squash...), and chop a big handful of fresh herbs (parsley, chervil, chives, rosemary, thyme, and/or coriander) and season to taste. Heat some olive oil in a deep baking dish or a round 10" cake tin, then pour in the batter, chuck in the roast veg and herbs, then cover with tin foil and bake at 250°C for 20 minutes. Remove the foil and bake another 10-15 minutes until firm.

-----------------------RECIPE INDEX-----------------------

Recipe Notes:
Tsp = teaspoon
Tbsp = tablespoon
1 cup = 250ml

With thanks to Active for publishing (and general encouragement), Steg for the cover design, Mikey, Charlotte and Hannah W for the writing contributions,
Jess at the Pod Cafe (www.facebook.com/ podcafefood)
for recipes, and my friends and housemates
for proofreading and recipe feedback ♥